EROTIC ASPECTS
OF
CHINESE CULTURE

by
Lawrence E. Gichner

This book is privately published for use and study by scholars in the fields of anthropology, and the social sciences, by physicians, psychologists and psychiatrists.

Published Part of this Study

    Erotic Aspects of Hindu Sculpture
    Erotic Aspects of Japanese Culture
    Erotic Aspects of Chinese Culture (constructive criticism requested)

In Preparation

    Examples of European Erotica (pertinent data invited)
    Erotic Art and Artifacts of the Americas
    Masterpieces of Erotic Humor

YANG AND YIN

Ancient Chinese philosophers sought to explain the universe in terms of two elemental principles or forces, from whose eternal and harmonious conjunction all things come into being. **Yang** is the male or active principle, characterized as warm, hard, dry, bright, procreative and steadfast; it is Heaven, sun, fire and light. **Yin,** the female principle, is passive, cold, wet, soft, dark and mysterious; it is Earth, moon and water. The joining of these forces is traditionally symbolized by a sphere representing the Great Absolute and divided into two curved sections closely entwined.

FILIAL PIETY

Longevity plays a dominant role in Chinese life and thought. It is believed that to the aged and enfeebled, mothers' milk, for those who can afford it, adds substantially to one's years, in spite of the fact that as a race the Chinese have a disdain for milk and milk products.

From his first breath a Chinese is taught respect for his ancesters and obedience to parents. Above love of country, to a Chinese, is his loyalty to family. In this ivory carving a mother is portrayed benignly giving succor to an old person before nourishing her own child.

Ivory carving without stand, 6¾ inches high.

Dedicated to

HAVELOCK ELLIS

Courageous scholar and dauntless pioneer who over
30 years ago inspired this research.

Of all the ten thousand things created by Heaven,
man is the most precious Of all the things that
make man prosper none can be compared with
sexual intercourse It is modeled after Heaven and
takes its pattern by Earth

Those who understand its significance can nurture
their nature and prolong their years: those who miss
its true meaning will harm themselves.

Tung-hsuan

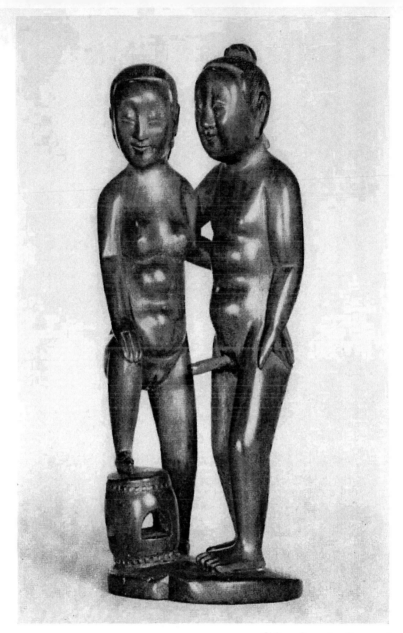

Ch'ing Dynasty, Boxwood

HAPPY COUPLE

The aesthetic difference between the Anglo-Saxon words nude and naked is aptly illustrated in this wood sculpture. Naked carries the implication of shame and discomfort, while nude connotes dignity, ease and pride in the human form which the statue of this happy embracing couple clearly conveys. The woman's traditionally bound foot rests upon a typical stool.

This wood sculpture is 5½ inches high.

TABLE OF CONTENTS

Introduction 9

Artistic Appraisal 11

Symbolism in Art 18

Taoist Concept of Sex Relation 20

The Prostitute's Code of Conduct 21

Random Notes 27

Purity of Literature 35

Sundry Remarks on the Classic of Medicine 41

The Classic of Medicine

     Part I 42

     Part II 49

     Part III 53

Introduction to Ching Ping Mei 83

Excerpts from Ching Ping Mei 86

Random Notes To Ching Ping Mei 115

The Lady of the Moon 120

Bibliography 130

DOLLS FOR DOCTORS

Graceful, exquisitely wrought Chinese nude female figurines of ivory, such as the one shown here, have a place of honor in many an art collector's display. Curiously enough, these nudes were designed to serve not only an esthetic, but also a very practical purpose.

Whereas, in the West, women have long since become accustomed to permitting complete examination of their persons by male doctors, the Chinese woman's traditional sense of modesty in this matter was much harder to overcome. Hence, Chinese doctors frequently had recourse to nude doll figures on which oversensitive female patients unwilling to allow direct examination, might point out the exact location of their affliction.

Ladies of high degree sometimes carried their modesty to the point of not even appearing in person at the doctor's office, instead sending a servant with a doll on which the location of the patient's discomfort was marked. The doctor made his diagnosis from this scanty information and prescribed what he surmised might be an appropriate remedy.

A tribute to the hardiness and endurance of **homo sapiens** is that the patient survived the physician's weird concoctions whose contents were not unlike the swill of a witches brew.

In some instances, a doctor might examine only his female patients wrist demurely thrust thru a curtain behind which she was concealed. Judging upon the rapidity and strength of the pulse beat alone a whole method of diagnosis depended.

Occasionally the vulva is indicated on these dolls by a thin line, but rarely is hair shown, for the Chinese did not believe with Dr. Oliver Wendell Holmes, who used to state to his Harvard students, that the **mons veneris** was the real **Arc de Triomphe**.

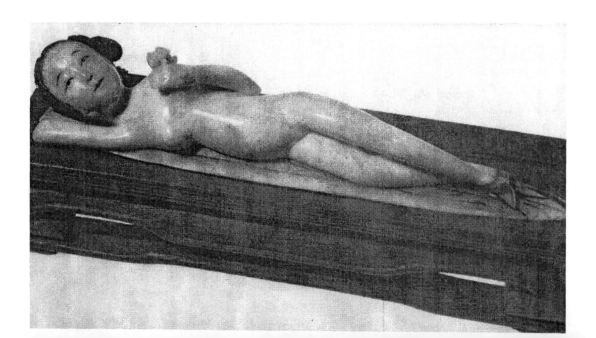

INTRODUCTION

The Chinese are different They are different in physical appearance, in social customs and likewise they are different from the rest of their fellow humans in their sexual behavior pattern.

If asked to characterize the sexual relations of the Chinese as they differ from other peoples of the world, the answer could be given by means of two simple thoughts which their Taoist philosophy emphasizes (1) marked prolongation of the act of copulation and (2) copulation without male ejaculation.

Ask the average citizen what he knows about the Chinese and his answer is startlingly scant, and the meager little he does know, on inquiry, develops into an erroneous concept, that the vulva of the Chinese woman is horizontal or transverse

To perpetuate this monstrous joke, modern photographs that have been "doctored" are circulated in an attempt to make a fact of fiction

So it sadly develops that what constitutes a great part of the knowledge of many so-called civilized people, about one-fourth of the earth's population, is a huge international hoax

How did this idea originate? How old is it? Who started it? One must search elsewhere than recorded history for the answer, for nowhere has your author been able to discover any printed source; yet it has been circulated throughout the world on the tongues of men, and is found in every civilized race

Some have volunteered the thought that the idea might have been suggested by the almond-shaped eyes of the Oriental, but it is simply preposterous to attempt to make a correlation between oval eyes and oval genitalia Where is there a connection?

It is in this very un-Chinese book about the Chinese that an attempt is made to throw some clear and serious light on the world's oldest, continuous civilization This book is un-Chinese in that its aim is to go quickly to the heart of the subject, and to present the essence of Chinese Erotica

The Chinese mind functions with the very reverse of this immediacy It abhors directness, and prefers to go the long roundabout way to arrive at its goal Experience teaches that what the Chinese say and what they mean have only a remote connection with each other. Such a mental process has produced a colorful and flowery style of speech, but in our age, where speed is an important element of life and man travels faster than sound, this technique of thinking presents many roadblocks to ready accomplishment.

To encompass the sexual life of the Chinese into a volume of these modest proportions is like compressing a horse into a bottle.

To have any significant value, it is important that we analyze clearly the core and then report concisely what is found

A study of this nature presents a recurring challenge to extend to the very limits ones' credulity and tolerantly to accept the fact that others can be different from ourselves, and yet in their own way be normal; i.e., that our behavior patterns can be as frighteningly strange to others as theirs may be to us

Westerners respond with marked consternation when told that a small foot has been a major source of Chinese sexual arousal; that the Eunuch by virtue of his physical disability rose to political power, that a plurality of wives and concubines, as well as of prostitutes, commingled in the same household with ready acceptance and with no racial prejudice; and that copulation without male orgasm was a practiced technique. These actions are so foreign to Westerners that they bluntly question their truth.

Coitus is a very ancient and basic function, not only of man but of a substantial portion of all living organisms, and it is questionable if anything new has been added to its expression for an inestimably long time. Though honeymooners and others may imagine they are discovering some unknown facet, the novelty is personal, not racial.

In general, facts, material and pictures in this study deal with the period prior to the Revolution of 1911 and the Communist regime that followed, since which time marked changes have taken place.

It is a long, slow, time-consuming process to make a study of this nature worthy and correct. It requires years of conscientious preparation to acquire an intelligent background of understanding of the culture and the people. For one has had to penetrate a double Chinese Wall, first, to break through to the Chinese themselves; second, to persuade them to talk at all on a topic they regard as taboo.

10

Are the novel positions illustrated in the pictures normal for the Chinese? If they were not used prior to seeing the pictures, they are afterwards; for the purpose of all books is instruction.

If a man did not try these "stunts" with his wife with whom he felt certain restraints, he did try them with his concubine or with a prostitute with whom he felt more free. He paid the prostitute for liberties; and she, to please the whims of her customer and to assure continued patronage, readily acquiesced. It must be remembered that prostitution is basically a business.

It is the new experience that is the exciting one particularly for the male, and it has been commented that "variety is the spice of wife." An oft-repeated and popular Chinese saying is "The thrill of one unusual act of copulation is equal to that of a thousand normal ones."

There never has been an accurate census of the Chinese. Authorities vary—but they do represent one-fifth to one-fourth of the world's population. To paint with a broad brush. and state they act "thus and so" is disastrous. In so large a. percentage of the human race, exception may be found to any statement, however true.

The intent of the author to write with finality and to present the complete picture and the whole truth is in reality, but a dream. If, with the erosion of time, it is found that instead of the whole truth he has found a few grains, he will be grateful and hopes the reader will share his gratitude.

ARTISTIC APPRAISAL

There are those who say Chinese art lacks quality. When judged by European standards this is true, and, by the same token, European art, judged by Chinese standards, is found wanting. The important thing is that Chinese art answered the esthetic demands of the Chinese. Art should be appraised by, and for, the people for whom it was intended.

Anatomical realism is not a factor in Chinese art, some critics argue. They contend that the artist was not a student of the human body nor did he attempt to make a factual representation. For a time, even days, he would observe what he wished to paint and then, returning home, would try to catch the spirit, not the detail, of what he had seen. Thus, his people sometimes lack the niceties of proportion to which

Western eyes are accustomed In essence one knows they are people, though the foreign observer may at first be confused by males with protuberant breasts, women wearing trousers, and men having a womanly appearance with their queues wrapped about their heads.

Thus the majority of Western authorities repeat **ad infinitum** that the Chinese were poor anatomists; never observed the human body and that, therefore, their portrayals were frequently only horrible distortions

However, in erotic art we find nudes that are skillfully rendered with fidelity and true understanding Regardless of how hard-pressed an artist may be for a model, he always has his own body readily at hand for study So it is believed that the poor rendering of the human form was not the product of ignorance, but of an artist's compliance with the tradition of prudery that forced him to incorrectly present the nude. Free from this tradition, he often did the human form full justice, as can be observed throughout these pages.

In much early Chinese art, nature is the dominant subject while man is but a minor part of the picture, which is his true proportion in terms of the universe

Judging the age of a picture can at times present its problems, for Chinese dress, like the Chinese house, has not varied for thousands of years In addition, old paintings can look very fresh and new from careful handling, and new ones can look old from rough treatment The artists of olden days worked on, or assembled, their pictures in a long paper scroll These scrolls were never hung but were carefully rolled up, carefully protected and preserved Only to please a specially honored guest were they, on rare occasions, brought forth and unrolled Then only a short section was shown at a time; and after the contents were absorbed, the scroll was progressively rolled further, presenting an actual moving picture of succeeding events.

Repressed by his Confucian teaching, no dignified Chinese would dare view erotic pictures in public, yet privately he had no hesitance in showing a series of illustrations dramatizing the facts of life to the ladies of his household, his girl friend or concubine.

This is just the reverse attitude of the Westerner who, though disinclined to show erotic pictures to his wife, would have no hesitancy about sharing them to friends.

It is characteristic of the Chinese to be reserved It is bad taste to exert oneself too much They are restrained; and part of their honorable behavior and noble manners is to observe things quietly, to be at ease and act calmly

The Chinese have strict rules of behavior It is considered bad taste to move too quickly, to express oneself too openly, to be very active He is a very self-sufficient person

One of the great psychological differences between the Japanese and Chinese, as reflected in their art, is that the Japanese love to show themselves in action, doing things; the Chinese do not Thus, a significant difference is reflected in the life and art of the people In Chinese painting, such as scenes of hunting, battle or street life, there is less vigorous movement and action than in Japanese art This is also true in their erotica, which shows a tremendous reserve.

White-skinned races say that the Chinese are emotionless creatures with impassive faces, and in erotic paintings they find the participants, especially the female, quite detached from the activity in which she is engaged The faces seem dull and soulless, devoid of all expression

Is this a true portrayal, as the artist intended, that the impassive female simply accepts passively, without response, the arduous advances of the male animal? Is this a true representation, in that the bride meeting and coming in contact with her husband for the first time on the bridal bed cannot feel any profound emotional response?

Or is it that Occidental eyes, untrained to the subtler innuendoes of the reserved Oriental, miss the gentler and more tender compassions that pass between the lovers? As ones' eye becomes accustomed to this shadowless art, he begins to see and sense in many instances that the portrayals do express deep feeling and profound emotion

But, it is important to remember that the Chinese artist is not concerned with personal characteristics The absence of expression in his subjects' faces does not disturb him The important thing to the artist is the individual's place in the external scheme of life Mountains, waterfalls and trees loom large in the Oriental picture, while man is a mere dot on the landscape His clothes may distinguish him as an official, a laborer or a fisherman, but any indication of the inner turbulence of the individual is often absent.

13

Artistic evaluation of an object is difficult, as appraisal varies with time, place and person. There are those who see in the unsigned creation—and none were ever signed—the hand of famous artists, while others evaluate them not as the work of artists but rather, of proficient artisans and skilled craftsmen. Whether the work of the great, the near-great or mediocre, one may with safety comment that some of the drawings are quite fine and done with an attempt to promote a quality that gave full dignity and beauty to the human body, and the function that was being performed

The restraint and conservatism of Chinese art is but a reflection of the restraint and conservatism of the Chinese way of life

Bustle and turmoil are considered barbarous, and the slow, plodding pace adopted through the centuries has become the accepted index by which culture and refinement are judged.

Thus, even in the erotic art expressions, there does not exist the violent haste and chase of the moment found in some other cultures, but a sense of poise, of leisure and of timelessness.

It must be remembered that this material, which was assembled from sources all over the world, was collected not on the basis of artistic merit, but rather in terms of the data and information that could be culled from every picture and each article. For years, we have had occasion to record and study Spring Pictures and marriage books in the leading libraries and museums of the world.

It is only when large quantities of material are assembled and examined that differences become apparent. When items are put together in cabinets and placed beside cabinets of other cultures in the family of mankind—as in the author's extensive private collection—then and only then do differences in behavior patterns become apparent.

In other cultures, there is portrayed an aggressive forcefulness on the part of the male, during courtship and intercourse, which is missing to a marked degree in the creations of the Chinese. The Chinese portrayals have about them a tranquil and restive playfulness—detachment from the business at hand—that render them distinct. When the study is pursued further, it is seen that this poise is a true reflection that underlies the Chinese philosophical concepts of coitus—to prolong the act by will with the aid of distraction of thought, gestures and at times of instruments

This study is not to index and classify on the basis of artistic value. The all-important fact is not that it is great art, poor art, indifferent art, or no art at all—what is of significance is what it says about the people and the direction in which they are going. How their sexual habits help us to understand them, and, in the process, ourselves, is of first importance

Research has been along three lines (1) extensive reading, (2) study of the art objects the Chinese created and (3) personal interviews with Chinese and those who have lived in the Orient

Chinese of the old school have been extremely reticent and non-communicative. They commented that sex was not a proper subject for a lady or gentleman to discuss.

Some ventured a little further and said they might look at the material I presented for comment for the purpose of the study, but not for fun. (Why not for fun?)

Others have frankly stated that they owned a collection of erotic items, and hoped their sons would likewise independently collect similar material, but to perpetuate the barrier of propriety they did not want to leave them their own collection

From other sources, it has been reported that the material is owned by wealthy men who have it hidden away, and show it only when, on rare occasions, they wish to bestow a special honor on a particularly esteemed friend. Because scrolls and pictures are stored away in chests and strong boxes, and are gotten out so seldom, very old pieces are today in a marvelous state of preservation.

It is the Chinese who have gotten out in the world and "rubbed shoulders" with other people to whom we are indebted for the greatest help, and a free flow of information. Cultured people of any race are a joy and enriching experience to encounter, to know and to have as one's friends

"The Tools of Heaven and Earth"

These remarkably life like dolls, with movable heads and arms, are fashioned of dried river mud, realistically painted. The tiny silken garments are removable, revealing bodies complete in every anatomical detail. The sexual organs, which are the source of life, are often referred to as "the tools of Heaven and Earth"—Heaven being the male, and Earth the female. The function of these dolls is believed to have been educational.

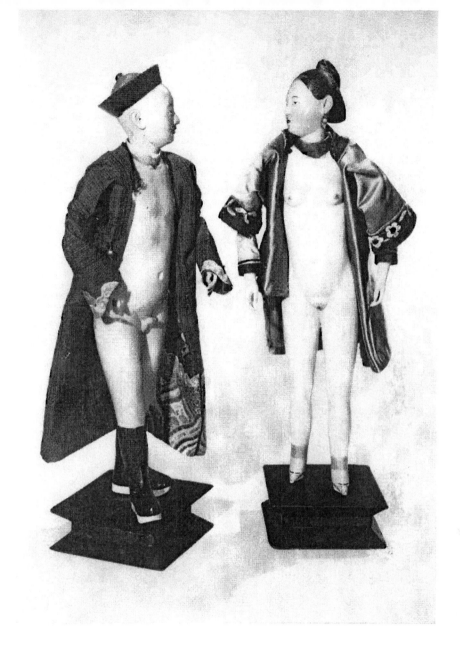

These dolls are to be looked at rather than handled, since their handmade clothes are of choice fabrics delicately trimmed with embroidery. Until recently Chinese dolls were made as much for adults as for children. They were objects of art rather than short-lived toys.

That these dolls represent adults is typical, for the child as a subject developed extensively only during the 20th century

When the prince of the royal household came of age he was taken to a temple and placed before a Tibetan **tanka** where, when the curtain was drawn, he saw "the facts of life" illustrated by one of the gods embracing his consort, or negative self.

17

SYMBOLISM IN ART

To the sensitive Chinese mind flowers, birds and animals had their symbolic meaning They represented a deeper significance than just that which met the eye Represented in art objects and decorated on a gift they had particular meanings. Symbolism plays a substantial part in Chinese art in whose development it found its finest development.

Fruit, listed in order of their esteem are the melon, peach, plum, prune and apricot. The melon both for taste and appearance is held in highest regard, and the "melon is broken" is a term applied to the breaking of the hymen These fruits, since their oval shaped seeds are similar in form to the external genitalia, are symbols of the female.

Guests who have attended parties of War Lords have described the great hilarity derived from bowls of fresh fruit placed in suggestive arrangement.

TREES

Peach—blossom suggests happy married life and is also the symbol of a pretty woman.

Willow—the deserted wife.

Japonica or Love Tree—twining branches symbolize married happiness.

FRUIT

Pomegranate—its many seeds cause it to be the token of a wish for a large family.

Plum—symbol of virility.

FLOWERS

Peony—regarded as the king of flowers; light, strength and masculinity.

Lotus—rising unspotted from the mud it betokens purity and creative power. The lotus seed pod symbolizes fruitfulness and offspring.

Chrysanthemum—suggests fidelity and constancy, blooming in spite of frost.

Wild Plum—snowy purity.

Orchid—noble men and refined women. Orchid pavilion is a poetic reference to the women's apartment and things connected with it

BIRDS

Wild Geese—Since it is said that a wild goose separated from its companion never mates again it is the symbol of married fidelity.

Mandarin Duck—married happiness and constancy, denotes a devoted couple It is said that when one duck passes away the other mate pines away and also dies

Nightingale—longevity and conveys the wish to a married couple that they may grow old together.

OTHER ANIMALS AND INSECTS

Butterfly—emblem of conjugal felicity and romantic love

Dragon—fertility.

Phoenix—signifies love and affection

Pair of Pekingese dogs—may husband and wife live together in united joy

Pair of Fish—fertility and conjugal felicity.

MUSICAL INSTRUMENT

Flute—represents marital bliss and suppression of lust.

FERTILITY SYMBOLS

Cowry Shell—used as early money, found in prehistoric graves, resembles vulva

Water—wavy line motif, meant a rich harvest and plentiful food and thus is related to fertility

Thunder—(spiral) like lightning storm and rain, it is a fertility emblem that would magically insure a bountiful crop.

Square—means earth, source of crops, signified fertility

Triangle—female pubic region, fecundity, appears in early art

Sun—(represented by circle) source of creation.

Gourd—(used for carrying liquid) associated with water, a prime fertility sign

19

TAOIST CONCEPT OF SEX RELATIONS

The Taoist believed the individual could achieve long life through correct breathing, exposure to the sun's rays, gymnastics and sexual activity Taoism taught that sexual relations nourished the body and aided in attaining an old age

1   The man had male essence, or Yin   The woman had female essence, or Yang   The one nourished the other, each was indispensable to each other.

2   The basic aim for the male was to conserve as much as possible his seminal essence.

3   During intercourse, his body was nourished by the orgasm of the female and strengthened by the retention of his own sperm

4   The female was not weakened by the loss of her lubrication

5   The male was weakened by the loss of his seminal fluid.

6   Sexual stimulus induces health and longevity, benefiting both the man and woman, sexual stimulus to be increased without the loss of seminal essence

7   Coitus with girls from 14 to 18 gave the man greater energy, while a woman of 30 and over had little essence left A man absorbed little strength from such contacts

8   Acts of intercourse with a succession of partners strengthened a man's vital powers   Orgasm was to be avoided and permitted only when children were desired.

9.   The male could prolong the act and preserve his sperm by performing a specified rythm, diverting his attention and thoughts

10.   If a man had an overpowering urge to ejaculate, he should first press his finger on the uretha between the scrotum and anus and cause the sperm to ascend in his body and nourish his brain.

11   By practicing reservation and ejaculating primarily when a child was desired, the results would assure a healthy baby.

Some believe that the practices of these techniques by the Emperors and others with a large household of women, provided a satisfactory sex life for both themselves and their lady-folk.

THE PROSTITUTE'S CODE OF CONDUCT

With the passing of centuries, certain phases of human behavior become firmly established and form the basis of an accepted etiquette Thus it is that the prostitute also has definite rules and niceties that standardize her relationship with her guest

1. On a first visit to a house of prostitution, a guest is introduced to all the girls Each girl greets him, bows respectfully and immediately departs She is introduced by her name, a nick-name or a number

2 A gentleman may invite to his room one, two, three or as many girls as his inclinations and purse allow, but a strict rule requires that once a girl has been invited, she is "your friend", and must receive attention on all subsequent visits to the same Sing-Song House .

3 .A guest is offered, for his refreshment, a steaming towel for wiping from his face and hands some of the earth's dust.

4. According to age-old usage, a servant brings him tea, melon seeds, and sweets or fruits to munch

5. If on a second visit a guest does not invite "his friend", this slight would make her lose "face" A good sing-song girl would not accept the company of another sing-song girl's "friend" A sense of solidarity is developed among the girls, and knowingly they would not break the rule by entertaining another girl's "friend."

6. One is not bound; however, to a sing-song girl forever, and the ethical method for ending such a friendship is frankly to tell the girl a change is desired The guest simply pays double the cost of refreshments served on such an occasion, and this ends all obligation to her

7 Delicacy does not permit the customer crassly to count out his money and pay it directly to the girl, but rather it is proper for him to slip the fee onto the same plate on which the sweetmeats were served.

8. It is against the custom to pay more than the established fee In simple terms, no tipping is permitted

9. Fees are split fifty-fifty between the girl and the owner of the house. The owner provides room and free board for his share of the "take".

Painting on Paper 6¼" x 8⅜"

FEMALE EXCITATION

This picture shows a girl aroused to masturbatory excitation by observing rabbits copulating. This concept can be quite erroneous as an indication of female response since this portrayal, like practically all erotica, is male conceived.

The male can be aroused by anticipation of the act, he can be aroused by observation of the act, he can be and is aroused by participation in the act, but none of these conditions are necessarily true in the case of the female who may remain quite indifferent to any and all of these stimuli.

22

10 (a) A thousand-year-old custom forbade a girl to accept an invitation to a meal

(b) She went to parties, was paid for her time, watched the men eat, but did not participate in the dining

(c) She served to enhance the occasion by the attractiveness of her presence, and not the size of her appetite

(d) She would lose "face" if she ate It would give the impression she did not have plenty in her home Her main duty was to provide amusing entertainment for her guest Sharing with him his food was considered a bother, not a pleasure

(e) Most sing-song girls were bought from their parents at a very tender age, and raised in the establishments where they worked At 14 to 16 years, they were already in the trade; and by the time they were 25 they were old, worn-out, and ready for replacement by younger recruits

EUNUCHS

Well documented pages record the history of the Eunuch; how he jockeyed himself into a position between the Emperor and his empire, controlled power, directed the flow of audiences, collected graft and "played his part upon the stage" of Chinese life The pages relate how, century after century, he gained, lost and regained position

Whether at the bottom of the social scale, as a criminal; or at the top as a court official, the role he acted is predominately that of villian—greedy, contemptuous and untrustworthy Whether the monstrous mutilation of his body warped him into an anti-social being or whether the idea once established, never changed, that he was a malevolent character is a question here raised for those who enjoy unravelling the threads of personality and setting them straight? Was the Eunuch cast into an unsavory role by historians because of their dislike of the abnormal or was he, truly, a diabolical creature?

Originally, castration was punishment By the Chou Dynasty, c 1027-256 B C, those so deformed had become attached to the Imperial household as servants in the women's quarters. Having close contact with the Emperor, they won his affection, moved into government, high position and power Court etiquette demanded that the Emperor be exclusive and seclusive The Eunuch in his position as go-between determined those persons and partisans the Emperor should or should not see, accepting substantial gifts in the process   By making such decisions, he was often the actual ruler, having the control of thousands in his palm.

This eunuch system, once established, was maintained; and law permitted the Emperor to employ 3,000 Eunuchs to discharge the functions of the palace—particularly to attend to the secluded Inner Palaces where resided hundreds of the Emperor's secondary wives, the Imperial concubines

As the throne was hereditary through the male line, the Eunuch was particularly entrusted with the supervision of the chastity of the many consorts   To avoid abuse of this trust, thousands of men lost their genitalia, so that the offspring of one man's genitalia could be correctly identified.   This was a preposterous example of fallacious reasoning that ended only with the inauguration of the Republic on February 12th, 1912— when the Eunuch System was abolished by decree.

Anti-erotic in itself, castration in the end catered to eroticism of the Emperor and various relatives of his royal house, who depending on rank, were allowed 10 to 30 Eunuchs

Surgery was usually performed before puberty, but also at times on married men with families who volunteered for service in the Court.   At first, recruits were drawn from the lowest strata of society, but later they were selected from above-middle-class families—those living particularly in the northeastern province of Chihli

The technique of surgery here outlined (1934) was related by one of the last of the Chief Eunuchs, Tse Yuen, of the then defunct Imperial Household

1.   The lad was first given a nerve-quieting herbal tea.

2.   Then he was tied firmly around the adbomen and groins to a wide wooden plank with head-end raised.

3.   His arms were strapped to a plank, and an attendant held his legs apart.

4.   A cloth was placed over the boy's face.

5   His genitalia was bathed with a solution containing hot herbs and pepper.

6   With a scimitar-shaped knife and one stroke the entire organ was swiftly cut away.

7.   A three-inch silver pipe was inserted in the urethra and powder applied to stop bleeding.

8   The wound was covered with absorbent paper soaked in cold water and bandaged firmly

9   The boy was released, supported under the arms by attendants, and walked for three hours

10   He was given no liquid food nor permitted to urinate for three days

11   After seven days the silver plug was removed, more healing powder was applied and the bandages were changed

In about a hundred days, the wound healed but soreness and loss of urinal control could continue for a year   During this period the boy was trained in Court etiquette

APHRODISIACS

The Chinese placed great credence in Aphrodisiacs   Scrapings of a rhinoceros or deer horn mixed in wine was esteemed, but ginseng was particularly regarded

Ginseng (Parax quinguipolea—Panax ginseng) was believed to possess magic potency for the prolongation of life owing chiefly to its fancied resemblance to the human form.   Its value increased in proportion to its age and similarity of shape to the human body   It was highly prized as an aphrodisiac and included as an ingredient in many medicines

Ginseng (spelt variously) has no official status in America having been completely eliminated from its pharmacopoeia, being likened by some as "the floor sweepings of an herbarium," yet ephedrine was used in China centuries before other cultures knew of its value

When China was opened to foreign trade, the Chinese supply of genseng (Jen Shen) was running low, but luckily for the Yankee merchants the root was found growing in New York along the Hudson Valley and in Kentucky near the Ohio River

Brides' Book

Part of the trousseau of the daughter of a cultured and well to do family was one box which contains the items for use on the bridal night. In the bottom of this box the mother, grandmother or an aunt slipped a book illustrating the intimacies of sex. In addition to education, it was considered by the superstitious as a protection which kept away the evil of both fire and foxes.

Here a young couple are examining the contents of such a book which would be the present day equivalent of a manual on sane sex life and sane sex living.

In the illustration the young couple are applying one of the lessons they have learned from the bride's book. The fan and porcelain pillow indicate that the time is summer. The picture is a water color on paper, and, typical of all erotic illustration, is executed in clear brilliant colors. Flowers, books, furniture and vases are at times executed with infinite delicacy and etherial charm thus emphasizing the aesthetics of the setting and ecstasy of the act.

Since the Chinese began by sitting on the ground on mats, and eating from low tables while occasionally supported by elbow rests, it was no great step to copulation on the ground, which so many pictures portray.

RANDOM NOTES

ART FORMS REPEATED

The epoch-making invention of printing made infinitely greater progress outside China than in the land of its birth Still to-day vast numbers of its teeming population can neither read nor write Therefore pictures play a significant role in education Down thru the ages, certain figures, by repetition, became stylized and were repeated over and over again Certain subjects based upon universal and ageless appeal, are as fresh today as they were thousands of years ago, and as they will be thousands of years hence The Chinese had no compunction about copying what pleased them, and felt in doing so they were paying a tribute, not plagiarizing Though they copied in spirit they never copied in detail, being sufficiently imaginative to make little changes of their own each time Thus, by copying the same subject and pattern from age to age it is possible, with a glance, to project oneself back into Chinese habits and customs hundreds of years thru the medium of the visual arts.

Popularity Of Vertical Postures

Bride's Book, Spring Pictures, or Wedding Scroll are all synonimous terms referring to a series of pictures that many centuries ago foreshadowed the continuous cartoon that likewise told an illustrated story.

Study of these pictures of copulation reveal that a goodly proportion of the couples are cohabitating while sitting or standing This preponderance of vertical positions, greater than in many other races, raises a question of why and in search for an answer the following are suggested:

1 The Chinese bed is hard, unyielding and mattressless, to be avoided when one seeks comfort

2 Women with "lily" feet can not be active bed partners since circulation has been obstructed by unnatural binding The large leg muscles become atrophied from disuse and the females ability to respond with reciprical movements is reduced

3 The male receives an erotic arousal from holding the woman's feet and this is most easily accomplished in a kneeling or standing position.

LOVE NOT MENTIONED

In this picture the gross distortion of the withered leg is worthy of note. Here the atrophied lower appendage and, in other illustrations, the extraordinary bulging of hips, which are man-induced deformities became signs of feminine beauty. In some pictures observers will note a projected and fat vulva which to medical men and anatomists, appear identical to that of an infant.

The delicate embrace of the woman, in the painting below, indicates a willing acceptance of her lover, although "love", in the Anglo-Saxon sense, was never considered respectable by the Chinese. For a man to say he "loved" a girl implied something irregular. For a woman to say that she "loved" a certain man would immediately lead to ostracism by respectable society.

Even after marriage, the sexual life of the woman was often repressed, and the conduct of those who had found their mutual love was aloof. The search, fumbling and finding which the youth of much of the world experienced, they never knew.

4. Orientals can squat on their haunches for hours at a time and centuries of adaptability make such a position not an obstacle.

KISSING

That the Chinese do not kiss is a popular misconception that is repeated again and again by otherwise well informed authorities. They do kiss, but the kiss is reserved for the intimate and seclusive act of cohabitation

Since some recording observers do not see people kissing in public, as in their own culture, they make the erroneous statement that the gesture is unknown

Not only do the Chinese kiss but they have developed it into a fine art in which tongue desirously caresses tongue, and wine is passed from mouth to mouth.

DOESN'T UNDRESS IN WINTER

In the colder regions of China winter lasts for six months and the people do not undress to either bathe or copulate There is no means of heating the room of even the most comfortable house Since he is afraid of getting cold the Chinese keeps on his garments when he goes to bed.

MALE MORE COLORFULLY DRESSED

As in the bird kingdom where the male is more brightly plumaged than the female, so the stronger sex, to show its superiority, reserves the privileges of elegance for itself.

CLOTHES

No field of study gives one the opportunity to study the clothes of a people quite so thoroughly as does that of erotica whose subjects run the gamit from dress to undress and undress to dress. In analysis one concluded the Chinese were never encumbered with the burden of a large wardrobe Their dress has not varied for thousands of years, thus making a mockery of fashion The difference between the garments of the well-to-do and of the artisan is a matter of material quality not of style

At no time does it appear that they wore underlinen or underwear.

Breasts

Large breasts were considered undesirable in unmarried girls and to avoid them they would bind their chests tightly. Mothers, believing in the old folklore that nursing mothers did not conceive, and also because of poverty, would nourish their children even unto the second and third year.

In many Chinese paintings depicting the sexual act, it is noticeable that the legs of the female, instead of encircling the male, are drawn up and back somewhat farther than would seem natural to people of other races. This has four probable explanations: first, that the Chinese normally possess a greater limberness of the joints than do Occidentals; second, the existence of a belief among some Chinese that only the genitalia, and no other parts of the body, should come in contact during copulation. This belief stemmed from the idea that the sensations were thus intensified. A third suggestion was that some Chinese abhorred close body contact and thus minimized it by having only the sex organs touch. A fourth, yet to be scientifically substantiated, is that these postures were necessitated by the position of the vagina which is lower in the body of the Chinese than in other peoples.

The breast received little attention in the early art. It was indicated but not the object of erotic interest until the advent of the Westerner in more recent times.

Thus in a happy scene, as shown in this four-inch-high porcelain couple, where a full breast is being fondled it denotes that the creation is without great age.

IVORY PENDANT

2⅛ Inches High

Heavy emphasis was placed on the birth of a male child. Not only did the arrival of a son raise the status and importance of the mother, but it also assured the continuation of the family name.

Thus, suggestively, little ivory carvings in the form of a young boy were fastened to cords of the marital bed or used as a pendant. To add realism the penis was so carved as to dangle loose and thus readily move back and forth.

Those areas which, in other parts of the world, are normally covered are not covered in children in China up to the age of four. The child is left to do what comes naturally because of the age-old difficulty—insufficient diapers to make continuous changes.

QUALITIES OF AN IDEAL GIRL

In the "Classic of the Virgin," it is stated the Ideal Girl for Intercourse possesses the following—

sweet character
gentle breasts
slow walking
soft black hair
smooth skin
her bones do not show
not too tall
not too short
not too broad
not too thick
high breasts
little pubic hair
each hair individual
not a tangled mass
juicy vagina
when you touch her vagina moisture flows
she can not keep her body still
she just naturally trembles
she can not hold herself back
she perspires easily
all of her movements respond to your actions
with this kind of girl you just act naturally
she is easy to satisfy so you will be satisfied too

WALLS

A student of erotology quickly becomes aware that a generous proportion of the scenes of copulation take place out of doors in strange and marked contrast to the housed seclusion-of-other civilized peoples. This fresh air mating with heaven as a witness is due to the building of walls, which perhaps more than anything else, distinguishes the Chinese from others.

A wall is as necessary to a city in China as clothing to a woman of the West When an emperor wished to punish a city, he would tear down its wall, leaving it naked. Every Chinese wants a protecting wall around his home

A Chinese proverb states that one act performed amid the tranquility of nature is equivalent to a thousand in bed.

Thus wealthy Chinese amid the walled seclusion of their garden could put into practical performance this pleasant philosophy.

31

Ivory carving done in either late Ming or in early Ch'ing Dynasty (1644-1912)

IVORY CARVED GIRDLE PENDANT

The fascination of ivory as a medium of artistic expression has lasted through the centuries, for it combines, in one material, several desirable qualities: it is enduring, and smooth to the touch, it lends itself well to fine, intricate workmanship, and of all materials it approximates most closely the human skin in color and surface texture.

The Chinese have proven themselves superlative artists in ivory, happily blending a keen aesthetic sense with deftness and infinite patience in execution. The works shown here are fine examples of ivory carvings of an erotic nature, which range in size from the almost microscopic to that of the illustration.

The two halves neatly fit together, conceal the interior, and form a gourd about which are covered flowers and an entwining vine. It was used as a decorative appendage that dangled from the end of a pipe or as a girdle pendant.

History of the Spring Palace

The whole field of erotica is given the name Spring Palace which supposedly dates from the Han Dyansty when Prince Kuang Chuan drew pictures of girls and boys in intercourse. After he made the drawings he invited his father, brothers, cousins, uncles and sisters to come together for a grand feast. After the feast he hung the pictures on the wall for everyone to see. This, it is reported, marked the beginning of the history of Spring Palace pictures.

In the Chi Dynasty an emperor painted spring pictures in his palace. He likewise had a banquet and invited high officials to observe his painting

In the Sui Dynasty, Emperor Yang built a mirror of shiny cotton and while having intercourse with his concubines observed her and his reflections in it.

In the Tang Dynasty Emperor Kao-Tsung built a house with many mirrors on the walls. One day he gave an audience to his Official Mr Liu who became shocked and rushed out to relate to his colleagues, "My goodness! There are many, many emperors in the palace Maybe they are spirits" In the next dynasty Empress Wu used this same setting of mirrors while having intercourse with her officials

CROSS DRESSING

That anomally of man and nature—the transvestite—was presented in the Celestial Kingdom as he was in the population of the rest of the world.

He painted his clean shaven face white, trimmed his eyebrows to represent a butterfly's wing, wore robes of fine silk, perfumed freely, flirted with his fan and travelled in an elegant blue palanquin lined with satin whose curved shafts raised him high above the ground.

A Clean Story

A very delightful tale is told about Ni Tsan, the great painter of the 14th century who had a pathological love of cleanliness not unlike those who are always and perpetually washing their hands He was spending one night with the courtesan of one, of his relatives and started by having her wash. Then he had her lie down and he smelt her body all over carefully.

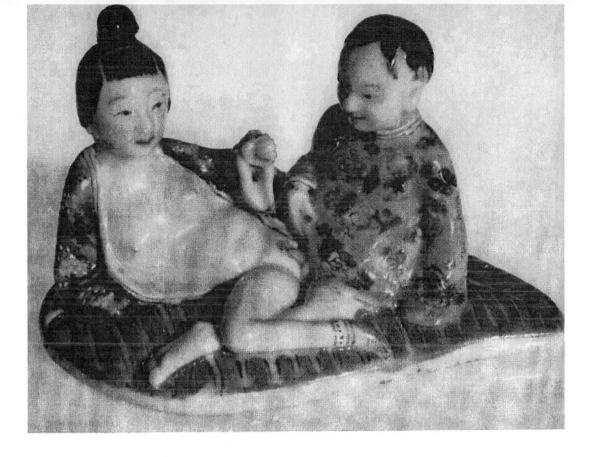

PORCELAIN FIGURINE OF A YOUNG COUPLE COPULATING

Many of man's behavior patterns are shaped by conveniences and comforts. Those accustomed their entire life to the luxury of mattresses, either with inner or outer springs, look with amazement at this seated couple, and others in a vertical stance.

They comment upon the "abnormality of the position", forgetting that many peoples of the world do not, nor ever have, reclined upon a mattress, but since life began, have adjusted themselves to hard floors and hard pallet. What is illustrated here is quite normal and quite natural to the young couple.

It must be remembered that the oriental has a limberness and dexterity in his legs made possible by a difference from the occidental, in his bone structure, at the junction of the leg and pelvis. This anatomical variation, plus the habit of aeons of squatting, which extended his leg muscles, gives him a greater flexibility below the waist.

Europe reached the height of her artistic genius by means of oil on canvas; while China reached her peak of artistic perfection with skillfully modeled and fired clay whose lustre scintillates with color, life and spirituality.

This intimately postured couple, a simple little piece, are seated on a broad leaf which occurs with frequency in amorous art. The leaf may be seen again in other illustrations. Some botanists identify it as a banana leaf, others disagree. No fruit is shown. It is thought to have erotic implications, but we have no present substantiation of this.

Some parts he suspected she had not cleaned thoroughly and he had her bathe again So the whole night passed in smelling and bathing, bathing and smelling, again and again with no consummation of the act, that was the purpose of their being together.

Months and years later, whenever Miss Chang related her experience with Ni Tsan she would end by collapsing with great laughter

Connubial Register

The Chinese, a cautious people, took no chances as to who was the correct heir to the throne With hundreds of imperial concubines and a plethora of children, intrigue and falsification could, in the fullest meaning of the term, presents itself as a real Chinese puzzle It was only natural that each consort was eager to bear the emperor a son so that she might be raised in status to the position of imperial mother

But chaos was avoided for not only was the sanctum of women, the "Inner Palace," heavily patrolled by some three thousand eunuchs, (more or less since precision in numbers was never a Chinese attribute), for what is little known is that it was the duty of the Chief Eunuch to keep a minute record of the Emperor's sexual life in which was listed the name of every concubine with date and time of her nocturnal visits

The emperor's problem of whom he should sleep with was simplified by the aid of a file system in which the name of every consort was listed on an ivory card, approximately one by ten inches The cards were kept in an appropriate holder in his bed room By rifling the ivories he could readily select a name from the deck and with a word to the Chief Eunuch the lady was ushered in

PURITY OF LITERATURE

The Chinese have many colorful names for the act of copulation and the genitalia which is, in part, due to the fact that traditionally nothing was said about sex, a subject on which they were very reticent Scholars had to submit their books to the Emperor for approval Other scholars read them, and if any vulgar terms appeared the author could be beheaded and his manuscript and books burned Thus the language was kept pure of improper terms Thus there flowered a language of beautiful symbolism

A sexual experience was never called a sexual experience because that would be coarse. It was not called something physical but "one spasm of cloud and rain." Clouds in motion at times appear like a man and woman engaged in the act. Clouds produce rain Likewise a man and woman as a result of the act give off moisture. Sometimes the act is spoken off as a "whiff of the spring wind."

Coitus was referred to in such poetic terms as—

Pleasure of Couch
Delights of Love
Amorous Combat
Playing heads and tails
Dew and water together
Wind and Willows
Flying with the wind and sporting with moon
Love birds flying shoulder to shoulder
A Couple of phoenixes behind the curtains
The mystery of clouds and rain (Billowy clouds
    entwining, representing the human forms which
    resolve into a rain of mingling semen and
    vaginal secretion)
Art of Yin and Yang (male and female, positive
    and negative)
Flowery Battle
Hidden Way
Art of the Bedchamber

Among these synonyms for the male member note the number of terms with reference to emplements of war—

Jade Sceptre
Staff
Weapon
Warrior
Positive Peak
Jade Stalk
Turtle's Head
Lotus Stalk
Sword
Spear
Great General

Since there are a far greater number of words and fanciful phrases descriptive of the female genitalia, and since most writing was done by the male, one can quickly judge where his greater interest lay

Jade Treasure
Heart of the Flower
Jade Gate
Precious Gate
Hidden Gate
Coral Gate
Female Gate
Grain-shaped Hole
Cinnabar Crevice
Golden Crevice
Jewel Terrace
Sacred Field
Female Door
Female Palace
Hidden Gully
Dark Vale
Mysterious pearl
Slit drum
Central point (old medical term)
Heart of the Peony
Dark part
Scabard
Dark Red Valley
Frog's Mouth

The Two Edged Sword

Liu Yen, whose religious name was Ch'un Yang-tzu, lived during the T'ang Dynasty (AD 618-906) and in a poem he referred to the vagina as a two-edged sword

Beautiful is this maiden her tender form gives promise of sweet womanhood,

But a two-edged sword lurks between her thighs, whereby destruction comes to foolish men

No head falls to that sword its work is done in secret, yet it drains the very marrow of men's bones

One thing there was, black-fringed, grasping, dainty, and fresh, but the name of that I may not tell.

MAXIMUM EXPOSURE

Pictures in a Bride's Book are often drawn with a maximum exposure of the sexual organs. Since the purpose of the books was instruction, emphasis is so placed that no detail be lost, but their consistent failure to indicate the clitoris proves the Chinese to be poor scientific observers.

Those having difficulty distinguishing between Japanese and Chinese erotica should learn one simple rule. The Japanese draw genitalia in Gargantuan proportions while the Chinese are comparatively normal and proportionally truer to life.

Though the Bride's Books are at times bound along one edge the older ones are accordion shaped with illustrations on only one side of each fold. They are called "books" and are book shaped yet it is rare for any to contain any reading matter. This is in all probability due to the general illiteracy which existed.

Great Repetition of the Same Positions

The Chinese with rare exceptions break away from routine. They incessantly revert to established types and familiar patterns. Therefore in coital posture there is comparatively little deviation from a few well established positions.

No Bound Books

Although China is the home of printing, the Chinese never learned the art of bookbinding. Erotic books, like others, are bound only in paper which for preservation are boxed in cloth-covered cardboard flaps These covered books are usually illustrated with scenes in which the scholar participates. See page 63

Disdain for Milk

The Chinese does not appreciate milk and never drinks it. Old men will consent to take some when enfeebled, and believe that mother's milk taken directly from the breast is best.

Chinese Attitude in the Ways of Life

1   Charm and beauty of the woman are not for public consumption, but attributes reserved for the admiration of the husband or lover

2   A woman does not lower her status by working.

3   The Chinese conform to a cultural pattern of emotional docility and social pliancy. They respond to a heritage of emotional control.

4   Under the influence of alcohol the Chinese seek seclusion.

5   They are a people who retreat into their surroundings

6   Sex is a natural expression of man which should be given expression at the right place, with the right party at the right time.

7   Sex expression is absent in general Chinese art and is concentrated almost wholly in erotica

8   Affairs of the heart were played down. A man married to have children, particularly a son or sons. His wife was selected by his parents to become a member of their household. Often he saw her for the very first time during the wedding ceremony If love came it was an after consideration.

9.   Singleness of devotion to one woman for all sexual activity was no profound concern A man while courting the great love of his life might without qualms or guilt complex engage in congress with other women or have homosexual experience without fear of social stigma or condemnation

Folk Sayings

ONCE IN THE FIELD OR ALONG THE ROADSIDE IS EQUAL TO A THOUSAND TIMES IN BED. (The heightened excitement of an unusual situation intensifies the pleasure many fold).

PROPER TECHNIQUE IS ONE TIME DEEP AND NINE TIMES SHALLOW (One of the secrets found in an old Chinese Classic).

ONE UNUSUAL COITUS EQUALS A THOUSAND IN BED.

OLD BULLS LIKE TO EAT THE TENDER GRASS. (Said of a father-in-law who covets his son's wife).

DO NOT DRINK ANYTHING COLD AFTER SEXUAL INTERCOURSE. (Doing so will bring a very serious illness).

SUNDRY REMARKS ON THE CLASSIC OF MEDICINE

During my years of study of the sexual behavior of the Chinese I had acquired bits of isolated knowledge here and there, but there was no deep and overall understanding

The folks of the Flowery Kingdom in this category of man's behavior were truly an enigma. I had the exhausting and frustrating sensation of attempting physically to push my way thru the Great Wall

Then one day I chanced upon five limp little paper bound volumes—Shuang Mei Ying An Ts'ung Shu containing The Sue Girls' Classic of Medicine—though the Chinese are given credit for having invented printing they never mastered the art of book binding—and set to work with my translator to rendering its pictographs into English

The saying is attributed to the Chinese that "One picture is worth 10,000 words" and when one does not understand Chinese, this is particularly true

This classic happily proved the Alladin's lamp to understanding that tied bits of isolated knowledge into a whole This was the key

Not only is sexual activity the source of life, but the manner of its expression is in itself a reflection of a way of life To understand a people we must understand their thinking The Chinese are serene, poised and philosophical That same calm and wisdom carries over in the intimacies of the bedchamber where heavy emphasis is placed on the prolongation of the act

What is the accepted science of one age and people is rejected as witchcraft by another. So in the light of the progress of hundreds of years there is much in the Classic of Medicine that is chaff, chatter and food for hilarity, but he who is sufficiently astute in life's experiences to divine that solid half in which lies the wisdom of the ages will find an abundance of practical and pungent material to enable him to express the natural forces with civility, grace and satisfaction, to act not as an animal but a cultivated human being—to respond not with impulse alone but also judgment.

It was a question of self-debate if the author should separate the applicable from the folklore and in brief, broad outline list the few rules to be followed to achieve man's age-old desire for indefinable pleasure indefinitely prolonged which the wily Chinese have known and kept secret. But, as in some schools of Chinese painting the artist does not say everything but leaves ample space amid his stalks of bamboo, willows and lofty mountains for the observers own meditations, so the reader is given the opportunity of experiencing the delightful satisfaction to discover, decide and select for himself where merit lies.

In addition to codifying the knowledge of the Chinese, the purpose of the book is a guide to a sane sex living not unlike the many being published in our time

The first book is in the form of Socratic dialogues of questions and answers in which Emperor Hwang, Mr. Peng Tsu, who has lived a long time, and the girls So and Huan are the participants

The old Chinese had no antipathy for long drawn out stories and seemed to enjoy repetition. To conserve time and space, and in condescension to the mania of the times for condensation, what follows is the essence, the unvarnished essentials

THE CLASSIC OF MEDICINE
(So Nu Ching)

Part I—The Secret Description of a Maid's Chamber

Part II—The Guide to a Maid's Chamber

Part III—The Book of Tang Hsian Tzu

Edited during the Tang Dynasty
618 A D.

Part I: Secret Description of a Maid's Chamber

To enjoy long life and good health, two things are essential. intercourse with young girls and retention of the sperm. Proper control of intercourse depends upon three qualities calm, inner peace, harmony with nature These create strong desire.

Roughness arouses no response; mutual stimulation produces pleasure. To rouse a girl, place the "jade-stick" gently inside her vagina, which will open for you. By gentle play, just inside or on the surface of the vagina, her emotions are aroused and she will desire coitus The girl lies on her back, her legs raised, the man stands between her thighs, kisses her mouth and sucks her tongue Holding his "jade-stick" in one hand, he touches the girl's vagina Slowly he inserts it With restrained movements, he quickly penetrates, slowly withdraws. When she begins to feel emotion, her body trembles and rises spontaneously to establish contact with his body. Now the man penetrates her deeply With closed mouth, the man, maintaining a steady speed, penetrates her nine times, finishing with the head of his "jade-stick" touching her clitoris. During this act, their mouths touch while they breathe together nine times.

The signs of pleasure in the girl, if followed as a guide, insure full pleasure to both parties. Penetration by the "jade-stick" should respect these signs: blushes—insertion, hardening of breasts—deeper penetration, perspiration of nose—deep penetration, swallowing of saliva—full penetration, vaginal flow—rapid movement of "jade-stick". Satisfaction at the climax is indicated by silence, imperceptible breathing, spreading nostrils, opening of mouth, tight embrace, moistening of clothes with perspiration, relaxation of muscles, closing of eyes.

The girl indicates her desires to her partner by ten signs: close embrace with body pressure—readiness for intercourse, separation of legs during intercourse—desire to have vagina rubbed, trembling of stomach—desire for climax and orgasm, trembling between anus and vagina—satisfaction, raising of legs with embrace—desire for deeper penetration, squeezing man's body with legs—excitement and pleasure, moving body from side to side—desire for similar motion of "jade-stick", raising of whole body with embrace of man—complete happiness, relaxation of legs and arms—end of orgasm, slipperiness inner and outer, of vagina—both have completed orgasm.

Nine Positions for Intercourse

1. Dragon Up—Woman beneath, penetration—eight shallow, 2 deep, in quick, out slowly.
2. Tiger Walking—girl on hands and knees, man behind—forty times in and out.
3. Monkey Fighting—girl on back with legs on man's arms who lifts her hips.
4. Locust Singing—girl faces ground, man holds her hips from behind, touches clitoris with head of "jade-stick". Insert six times, then nine, six and nine, repeat as often as possible.
5. Turtle Jumping—girl sits with legs bent, man presses her feet to his chest. Penetration. Press clitoris at depth of penetration. Girl should enjoy, man should retain his sperm.
6. Flying Phoenix—girl lies face up, man lifts her legs and kneels between, resting weight on hands. Penetrate deeply to press clitoris. Deep and slow penetration three times, deep and quick eight times. Repeat as

often as possible. Girl's vagina and rectum should tremble.

7. Rabbit Nibbling—man lies face up, girl straddles his legs, facing his feet, her hands on the mattress. She rubs upper part of vagina with his "jade-stick" until her "lubrication" flows. Girl places "jade-stick" and rides up and down like a rabbit nibbling.

8   Sliding Fish—man lies face up, girl lies on him, face to face. She holds "jade-stick", puts it into herself slowly. Moves forward and backward, like a fish swimming.

9. Love Bird—man sits upright, legs slightly bent. Girl straddles thighs, face to face. Girl embraces man, inserts "jade-stick", which must touch her clitoris. Girl embraces man with both arms, man holds girl's hips and helps her to move up, down and to sway from side to side.

EIGHT BENEFITS OF INTERCOURSE

1   To secure control of ejaculation during intercourse—assume normal position of intercourse, penetrate two shallow, nine deep, repeat several times a day during fifteen days.

2   To procure even temper in a man, a warm vagina in a woman. Woman lies face upward, hips on a small pillow, man inserts his "jade-stick" three times shallow, nine times deep. Repeat several times, three times per day, for twenty days.

3. To increase a woman's facility for intercourses. Woman lies on her side, legs bent; man, at right angle to her, penetrates four times shallow, nine times deep and quick; repeat. Four times per day for two days.

4   To cure aching bones and muscles in a woman. Woman lies on her right side, bends left leg, man raises her left leg, penetrates five times shallow, nine times deep and quick, repeat. Continue five times per day for ten days.

5   To insure regular menstruation—Girl lies on her side with right leg bent, man on floor, holds right leg, penetrates six shallow and slow, nine deep and quick, repeat. Continue six times daily for twenty days.

6. To cure anaemia—Man lies face up, girl straddles his legs and inserts "jade-stick". Girl regulates penetration—seven times slow and shallow, nine times deep and quick, repeat. Continue seven times per day for ten days.

7. To strengthen flow of vagina "lubricant"—Girl kneels or bends, man penetrates from behind, nine times shallow

and slow, nine times deep and quick, repeat   Continue nine times per day for nine days

8   To cure vaginal odor—Girl lies with legs bent, man penetrates nine times shallow and slow, nine times deep and quick   Reverse positions, girl completes same cycle   Continue nine times per day for nine days

SEVEN DANGERS OF INTERCOURSE

1   When a man forces himself to have intercourse without desire, he will perspire freely, his heart becomes weak, his eyes will not open easily   To cure these, or any other illness, do as follows Girl lies face up, her legs resting on man's shoulder, his hands on the mattress Girl's hips will be raised   Girl performs movement, man retains his sperm   Repeat nine times a day for nine days

2   Intercourse after overeating or drinking produces dry mouth and fever, premature ejaculation in intercourse   Cure Girl lies face up, left leg slightly raised   Insert "jade-stick" one and one half inches   Girl performs movements, man retains sperm   Repeat nine times a day for nine days

3   To strengthen penis when erection is not sufficiently firm for satisfactory intercourse   Rest for two weeks then follow directions below   Girl plays with genitalia to arouse desire. She lies face up, embraces his hips with her legs, inserts "jade-stick" a short distance, shakes her hips with up and down movement. Man retains his sperm   Repeat nine times per day for ten days

4   To cure fatigue, excessive perspiration, dry and bleeding lips cause by frequent intercourse   Man lies face up, girl faces his feet with her hands on the mattress, she inserts his "jade-stick" half its length, moves up and down, from side to side   Repeat nine times per day for ten days.

5   To cure excessive flow of urine, trembling, dizziness, flow of tears caused by intercourse   Man lies face up, girl facing him, inserts "jade-stick", moves up, down, sideways   Repeat nine times per day for ten days

6   To cure excessive vaginal flow with crystallization, fatigue caused by intercourse, continual thirstiness   Man lies face up, girl lies on him, face to face, with hands on mattress   She inserts "jade-stick", sways, moves up and down   Repeat nine times per day for ten days

7   Exhaustion of blood and of energy, roughness of skin, itch-
      ing testicles caused by overindulgence of intercourse
      Girl lies face up, pillow under hips.   Man kneels, inserts
      "jade-stick" quickly and deeply   When girl shakes and
      trembles, man ejaculates.   Repeat daily for ten days.

BENEFITS ACCRUING
from Retention of Sperm

Retention of sperm during intercourse induces general good
health and happiness   Benefits accrue in the following order
first time—lungs are strengthened, second—eyes and ears, third,
all illness of both partners disappears, fourth, general peace of
mind and body, fifth—circulation of blood will improve, sixth—
backache will disappear; seventh—hips and thighs will become
strong, especially for intercourse, eighth—skin becomes smooth,
pimples disappear; ninth—long life, tenth—you are a superman

The "jade-stick" as an index of health

1   A firm, hot penis from which the sperm spouts congealed
      indicates general good health.   A soft penis with a
      weak flow—energy low
2.   Watery sperm in deficient quantity—poor muscle tone
3.   Malodorous sperm—arteries ailing.
4   Flow of sperm without ejaculation—bone tone poor.
5   Soft "jade-stick"—general bodily weakness.   The general
      cure for the weaknesses indicated above· intercourse
      daily for one hundred days without release of sperm.

Dangers arising from intercourse at the wrong time or place

1.   If at noon or at midnight—child will be deaf and dumb.
2   During a solar eclipse—child will have malformed limbs.
3   During thunder and lightning—child will be insane.
4.   Lunar eclipse—mother and child will die.
5.   When rainbow is in the sky—child will bring bad luck to
      the entire family.
6.   During winter or summer solstice—child will harm both of
      its parents
7   On the first day of the month if the moon is dark, on the
      fifteenth of the month if the moon is full—the baby will
      be a rebellious child.
8.   If after excess of food or drink the child will be paralyzed

46

9 After a hot bath, after a long journey on foot, when fatigued—avoid intercourse
10 Intercourse undertaken on May 16 will bring death in three days

To insure a healthy baby be sure that the mind is at peace Do not overindulge in food or drink Between midnight and dawn three and one half days after the woman's menstruation is a suitable time Play with the girl until her desire is aroused At the moment of ejaculation make sure that the "jade-stick" rests between her clitoris and her vagina, if penetration is too deep, sperm will not enter the womb

CHARACTERISTICS OF AN IDEAL BED-MATE

Good temper, bright eyes, gentle voice, soft hair—if dark, the darker the better—smooth skin, limbs moderate in length Vagina relatively free of hair, placed high rather than low During intercourse she has a plentiful flow of fluid, her body trembles and shakes, at climax she perspires a little

LOVE SICKNESS

Sexual desire frustrated of fulfillment creates dreams of intercourse Secret, unexpressed longing will result in death if the dreams are allowed to continue The cure for this illness is intercourse during which the man retains his sperm. If the man has become weak, he places his "jade-stick" in the girl's vagina and makes no motion Where the lady is of noble birth so that her parents will not allow her intercourse with her man, her illness may be cured by an application of warm stone sulphur to the lips of the vagina and a decoction of deer horn in hot water, taken internally Young deer horn is the only tonic to enable young men and women to sustain prolonged intercourse over a considerable length of time, without danger to the health

A preparation of young deer horn taken three times daily for twenty days is a cure for impotency

METHOD FOR FEMALE MASTURBATION

Symptoms of need. If woman of thirty perspires, loses appetite, suffers itching vagina, feels constant sexual desire the following is the indicated remedy Mold dough in the form of a "jade-stick", bake it, cover it with fine silk Insert this in her vagina, withdraw, repeat from twenty to thirty times.

47

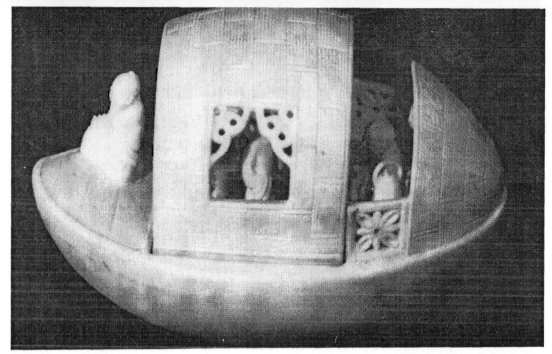

FLOWER BOAT

White Ceramic Boat with removable section that reveals copulating couple on bottom. Fine and delicate workmanship.

A whole world of Chinese are born, eat, sleep and die on board junks. Legend says that during a lifetime some people never touch shore. Amid a community of boats there are special junks that serve as wedding chapels, there are those that likewise function as houses of prostitution, whose interiors are elegantly finished in carved and gilt wood and furnished with chairs and stools all made of ebony and rosewood with marble tops.

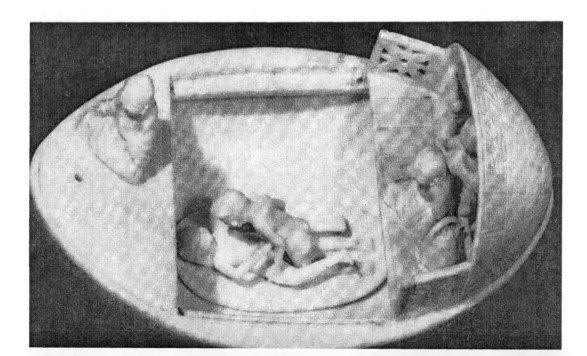

PART II—THE GUIDE TO A MAID'S CHAMBER

Peng Tsu raised the question How could the Emperor Hwang have intercourse with 1200 women, remain healthy, and become an angel in heaven? His own answer was. He followed proper methods and enjoyed only girls who were young, with no mother's milk, and who were sufficiently fat   Seven such girls are sufficient, but the more the better.

He continued his discourse by saying that a man should know the principles of intercourse. His mind should be tranquil   Arouse the girl to passion by kisses and caresses, when her ears and cheeks become warm, her breasts firm and erect, caress them   When her neck and shoulders tremble and her legs become restless, she willl want to embrace the man's body. Then, touch the vagina with the "jade-stick" and insert it gradually.   A girl's tongue and her saliva are good for the health If, during intercourse, her saliva be swallowed, it will cure indigestion and assure smooth, healthy skin.

Lau Ching, a Taoist, confirmed Peng Tsu's remarks and added that too rapid movement was unhealthy   Twenty sessions without an orgasm will cure all sickness and assure long life. Orgasm will spoil everything.

The Classic of the Angels advised that intercourse with ten different girls in one night was good if the sperm be diverted to nourish the brain.   This is done as follows when you feel the need for orgasm, press firmly, with two fingers of the left hand between the anus and the penis, raise the head, inhale deeply, chatter the teeth together.

The greatest benefit from intercourse may be realized as follows open the eyes widely, look around. You can live to the age of two hundred with a youthful complexion, good color and no pimples

The Art of Intercourse

The secret should be kept from the girl for she may not co-operate   Young girls, between the ages of fourteen and nineteen are the best   If the woman is over thirty, with a child, you will gain nothing   Numbers are important three, six, nine or eleven girls are best, but the more the better.

If you divert the sperm to the brain, the skin will be smooth and shiny, the body light, the eyes bright, energy plentiful—an old man will look like a twenty year old

Variety benefits both men and women   A Taoist stated that change benefits girls, one girl served by one man becomes thin and weak and dies early.

49

In intercourse, the girl should have her orgasm first, so that her nerves will be rested and calm Otherwise she will complain and feel unsatisfied Both partners will suffer ill health and feel half-sick otherwise.

Mutual Benefit from Intercourse

With proper knowledge, man and woman benefit, he from her lubricant, she from his sperm With proper methods they can live for nine days on intercourse alone, without food. The principle factor do not let the sperm ejaculate Hold your sperm for twenty days—this will cure all illness During intercourse close the eyes, otherwise you will suffer eye trouble

What to Avoid During Intercourse

During intercourse the following are to be avoided· 1) constant use of the position in which the girl lies on her back with her feet up, reverse this from time to time to avoid pains in the waist, 2) placing the head too low on the bed, rest the forehead on that of the girl to avoid stiff neck; 3) intercourse before midnight when digestion is still incomplete; 4) intercourse during drunkenness to prevent too great a waste of energy, 5) intercourse with a full bladder since this causes difficulty in urination, an itching penis, and pains beneath the navel, 6) intercourse if you suffer from boils, this causes piles

Benefits to be Secured from Intercourse

1. To secure brightness of the eyes, prevent orgasm by lifting the head, inhaling with little noises, open wide the eyes and look to left and right, contract the muscles of the lower belly and the sperm will return to the blood

2. The method of nine times shallow, one deep benefits both partners—shallow touches the clitoris, which benefits the man, deep touches the uterus, a benefit to the woman If mouths are joined, the man benefits from the girl's breath Repeated nine times, both benefit. To do this, remove the "jade-stick" when it is hard, when it has become soft, replace it—both you and the girl will last longer

3. Impotence in a man can be cured if the girl, lying on her back, separates her legs about nine inches, while the man applies his mouth and tongue to her vagina swallowing her lubrication Then he uses his finger, next his "jade-stick", to touch her clitoris and arouse her desire In spite of his own desire, he should not ejaculate Repeat nine times shallow—

50

one deep for ten days Then his "jade-stick" will become as hard as iron and hot as fire, fit for intercourse with a hundred girls.

Dangers of Intercourse

Unless the proper precautions are observed, children will suffer at conception, as the following table indicates

1. on the first or the fifteenth of the month—weak limbs
2 during a wind or sand storm—swollen limbs
3 during drunkenness—mental disturbance
4. within half an hour of father's urinating—indeterminate sex
5 when father is fatigued—unhealthy, die young
6 immediately after a hot bath—physical or mental weakness
7. when father has muscle or backache, or worried—child abnormal
8 before the New Year—child will be deaf and dumb
9 with lights too bright—death from hurts
10. during a period of mourning for grandparents—attack by fox or tiger in later life.
11 while the sun is going down—irrational speech
12 at noontime—epilepsy

How to Have Healthy Children

1 To have a clever, intelligent, long-lived boy or beautiful, gifted girl who will marry well—
   a) do not release the sperm too frequently,
   b) wait at least three days after the mother's monthly period,
   c) have intercourse just before sunrise

2 Difficulties arising from age
   a) children of a centenarian will be short lived
   b) a man of eighty years, with a wife of eighteen, can produce normal children
   c) a woman of fifty years, with a young husband, can have healthy children

3 If a woman, three months pregnant, burns the insignia from the hat of a civil or military official and swallows the ashes with wine, her child will be clever, rich, noble This is a secret for men alone to know

51

4   A childless woman can insure pregnancy by holding twenty-seven soy beans in her left hand, in her right her husband's "jade-stick" which she inserts. During intercourse she chews the beans, at the moment of ejaculation she swallows them.

5.   Intercourse with a girl of good character, not too fat or too thin, too short or too tall, whom you love, will insure health and long life.

When a man's desire is greater than the woman's, and his sperm is greater in quantity than is her fluid, the child will be male; if the reverse is true, female. Avoid girls who are ugly, who have irregular teeth, whose necks, or whose vulvas have too much hair, or if the vulvar hair is too long. Avoid girls with hairy arms and legs. A jealous girl will let you have no peace. Cool girls are weak, shun those whose vagina is cool. Girls with body odor, especially under the armpits, should be avoided.

Literature

Chinese literature is extensive. With excerpts here presented from the Classic of Medicine and Ching Ping Mei, we have excellent samplings of the Chinese sexual knowledge and thought.

In the Sung period (11th and 12th Centuries) highly erotic tales were recorded and appear in an anthology of stories known as **Chingpen T'ungshu Shiaoshou.**

Soo-Yu-Kin, Plain Girl Gospel, is a classic erotic novel written within the last 500 years, but claims of greater age are made for it. It gives intimate details of what lovers do when given a chance, but some of the descriptive terms are unintelligent to present day scholars.

Novels were not classified under the four great divisions of literature, and therefore they were not regarded as an integral part of the literature proper, but especially during the Ming Period (1368-1644) many first-rate love stories, frank and uninhibited, appeared, which must not be overlooked by students of life and human behavior.

The puritanical counsels of Confucious (551-478 B C) exerted a powerful influence in suppressing erotic literature and keeping it an undercover commodity, but as a very basic expression of man, its creation, as here proven could not be denied

PART III—THE BOOK OF TANG HSIAN TZU

In the whole world man is supreme over other beings because he knows the art of sexual relationships while the other animals can not understand the art of intercourse A person who understands the art of intercourse will have a long life, If he does not he will die early

The girl must react to the man's stimulus, If the girl does not respond no good can come to either man or girl When a man thrusts the girl must push up in response, doing this, the world will become peaceful

Intercourse should start by the girl sitting on the man's right with his arm around her and his hand touching her arm and breast with alternating firm and gentle caresses The man kisses by holding her lower lip and she by holding his upper lip, they suck each other a little and nibble each other's tongue Sometimes the man plays with her ear or caresses her head With this preparation, the girl's worries vanish; her desires increase and her hand reaches for the Jade-Stick while the man touches her vagina As a result, his jade-stick becomes hard and her vaginal lubrication flows, and the natural desire for intercourse is aroused Omission of this preparation will prevent harmony of feeling

After the girl lies down and spreads her legs, the man should kneel and caress the outside of her vagina with his jade-stick just as a cedar tree blocks the entrance to a cavern By kissing the girl's mouth, biting her tongue, looking her in the face, or kissing her nipple— he will sufficiently arouse her desire, then the man inserts the jade-stick a little way, first to the right, then to the left, finally to the center; then shallow and then deep penetration to full length, ending with a circular probing This will make the girl feel very happy at first and finally as if dead When she is speechless, take out the jade-stick and wipe off her lubricant with a piece of silk, then re-insert it Both should take a short rest Then nine times shallow and once deep, to the right and to the left side three times. If one can control oneself, repeat this rhythm twenty-one times This will cause the girl's whole body to vibrate and make her gasp Then let the spirit flow while the penis moves in a circular pattern. This will cause both partners great happiness.

Painting on Silk

THE HELPING HAND

While Westerners, mostly the female, feel the presence of a third person is a violation and intrusion upon their privacy, this servant makes herself useful by helping the gentleman sway forward and back, thus delaying his orgasm and preserving his essence.

Books, pen holder and brushes placed on a table in the room inside the window indicate the gentleman is a scholar.

It is well known that increasing the tempo of the pelvis motions can speed the arrival of the spasms or orgasm, and or, conversely, retarding the vigor and rapidity of movement cause delay. Here, thanks to the leverage furnished by the young servant, dressed in typical stomach-covering vest, the involuntary convulsions are retarded, and the duration of copulation is increased. Taoists wrote treatises on the sexual act which suggested that prolonging the performance extended life and promoted good health.

THIRTY POSITIONS

1 Common—girl below, man above

2 Roving Around—man moves his penis with a circular motion

3 Two Fish Biting—both kiss while copulating

4 Horn—like buffalo horns interlocked—their arms are around one another

5 Twisted Worm—with her arms about his neck and her legs about his body they twist like worms.

6 Dragon Dance—the man holds one of her legs over her breast—her other leg is free

7. Facing Fish—man and woman on their side, facing one another, woman puts leg across man's hips

8 Two Pheasants with one Heart—Girl lays down with spread legs while man holds her neck, his arms encompass her waist

9 Two Fighting Birds—man kneels between girl's legs while holding her by the legs, girl resembles bird fighting as her legs move

10 Mandarin Duck playing—girl lays on her side with both legs to the side of his body, man puts jade-stick between her legs

11 Butterfly flying—man lays down, girl sits on him, he holds her as she flutters up and down

12 Birds in Opposite Flight—man lays down, girl sits on him, facing his feet (also called Shrimp)

13 Fallen Cedar Tree—Man stands while girl rests her legs on his shoulder as he holds her waist Her legs move like the branches of a tree

14 Standing Bamboo—Man and girl stand embracing each other

15 Dancing Birds—girl lies on the bed, legs raised, while man, seated, has intercourse

16. Large Bird and Small Chicken—Large woman lies down while short man has intercourse

17 Flying Sea Gull—man sits on the edge of the bed his feet on the floor the girl's legs resting on his arm Together they have intercourse Her legs, moving, resemble the motion of the wings of a flying gull

18 Jumping Wild Horse—girl lies on the edge of the bed, man stands, her legs rest on his arms or shoulders

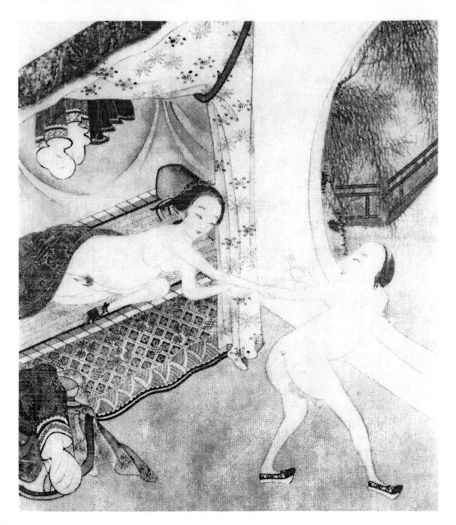

A THWARTED ESCAPE

This unsatisfield Chinese Potiphar's wife catches her tired lover as he anxiously tries to depart thru the moon door, indicating with his raised fingers that two performances should be sufficient.

Thru the medium of erotica one sees into the intimacies of the Chinese home and bed, here completely enclosed on three sides by decorated curtains which are here drawn to one side. The silk clothes of the lover he limply throws over a round stool while the lady's garments hang within the curtains.

Silk was a luxury never accessible to the masses. It was worn by the wealthy who could afford its costly fragility and was used more by men than by women. Since the loosely draped clothes we see in erotica are predominately silk, we can easily deduct the people represented possess wealth, for the masses wore nothing better than calico.

The thin pallet laid over the bed strings leaves much to be desired in comfort in the estimate of those westerners who are accustomed to the more resilient comfort of a thick mattress.

19 Racing Horse—Man kneels while the girl lies on the bed with one leg on his shoulder, his hand holding the foot of the other leg

20 Horses Shaking their Feet—While the girl lies on the bed, the man holds her extended legs by the ankles

21 Jumping White Tiger—Girl kneels, her head against the bed while the man inserts his jade-stick from behind Her white body moves like that of a jumping tiger

22 Locust on the Tree—Girl is face down on the bed, her hips raised, the man's legs are stretched out beneath her body His body is the tree, she is the clinging locust

23 Playing Mountain Goat—man seated with outstretched legs, girl seated, facing in same direction She kneels; puts in the jade-stick and observes its action When they move the girl resembles a playing goat.

24 Fighting Cocks—man seated on the bed holds girl, facing him, on his lap A second girl kneels beside them and helps insert the jade-stick During the action she helps in pushing their bodies together (in a manner somewhat reminiscent of an accordion player with his instrument)

25 Bird in the Cavern—girl sits, holding her legs raised by the ankles, the man kneels to insert the jade-stick

26 Large Flying Bird—the girl's legs rest in the crook of the kneeling man's arms

27 Singing Monkey Holding Trees—man sits on the bed, the girl, facing him, straddles his waist while her hands embrace his body With one hand the man helps the girl move her hips while he props himself up with the other

28 Playing Cat and Mouse—girl stoops, man, standing behind her, holds her hips

29 Jumping Mule in Spring Time—girl stands, her hands on the bed, man approaches her from behind

30 Playing Dog in Autumn—both are bent over, rump to rump (like caught dogs) facing in opposite directions

In addition to the material given above, the following subjects are treated

1 How to control orgasm
2 How to have a boy or a girl baby
3 The proper direction to face during intercourse
4 Medicine for a weak Jade-stick.

Appendix—Happiness from Intercourse (poem).

VISUAL STIMULANTS

Animals or fowl in the act of copulation appear frequently in erotic pictures, presumably acting as stimuli to the lovers who cast side glances at them while engaged in their own pleasure. A pair of chickens supplements the amorous scene pictured on the inner panel of this **Ch'un Feng.**

Usually a set of **Ch'un Feng** was composed of six or twelve double panels, all encased in a box beautifully covered in brocaded silk. The panels themselves, done in low relief, display fine and delicate craftmanship of the type known as Peking Inlay or Peking Ivory. Ivory is used to represent flesh, with lacquer, stained bone, mother of pearl, jadite, and tinted soapstone artistically combined to form dress, furniture, shrubbery and other details. The background is painted.

As a culture becomes more sophisticated, sex is often concealed behind a conventional disguise. Chinese art had produced a variety of such disguises, among them what are known as **Ch'un Feng,** or Spring Palace, panel pictures, two examples of which are illustrated here. The outer panels normally exposed to view are decorated with ordinary, commonplace subjects, but they slide upward to reveal inner panels depicting erotic scenes of husband-and-wife intimacy or lovers caressing.

The name **Ch'un Feng** derives from the fact that spring is traditionally the season of love's awakening, and from the customary setting of the amorous scenes of the panels in the ornate interior of a regal palace or wealthy mansion. In some parts of China **Ch'un Feng** were placed among the belongings of a bride-to-be, and sometimes of her husband, to serve as a guide in sex education and key to marital felicity.

Size 7⅝" x 9⅜"

MONGOL LOVE-MAKING

Scroll Painting on Silk

Sweeping southward from the Siberian plains, the nomad Mongols conquered China in the 13th century. They were accomplished horsemen, as agile and hardy as they were cruel and destructive. When food was unobtainable, it is said that they sucked the warm blood of their horses and rode on to conquer and pillage.

In view of the Mongols' unequalled skill in equestrian acrobatics, it it natural enough that the Chinese artist who produced this masterful scroll painting should have incorporated this talent in a rather fanciful picturization of Mongol sex **mores.** The scroll is 8½ inches wide and 6 feet 9 inches in length, portraying ten scene of love-making both on horseback and off. Sections of the painting are reproduced here.

Unlike the Japanese, whose mastery of wood-block printing made of pictures a means of communication for the masses, the Chinese laboriously made each picture an original hand painting, which greatly increased cost and reduced scope of circulation.

Since no pictures in this phase of art was ever signed, it is difficult to determine which is original. Scrolls were copied and re-copied, yet the artisans who worked on them were sufficiently talented and imaginative to make such minor variations that no two scrolls are identical reproductions.

In some instances, paintings were produced by the factory method with many workers busily working in one large room. Young children were employed, who acquired an early dexterity and skill in creating the subtlest shadings and most elaborate detail.

Peking Inlay

Scholar Esteemed

In few countries was the scholar so highly regarded and respected as in China. He was the true aristocrat; at the top of the social scale. To be born of poor parents was not a handicap to advancement. A retentive memory for the Four Books of Confucius and the ability to write poetry were essential to political success.

In erotic illustrations the scholar appears with marked frequency as a lively contestant in love's bouts. Living a sedate life, his sexual activity was

socially accepted as legimate release and an expected part of the little exercise he performed. His occupational implements—books, pen holder or brushes—are often shown ever close at hand. Pens, paper, ink and inkslabs are called the "four precious things."

However, it was often only sons of the wealthy Mandarin class who could afford the luxury of leisure necessary for scholarship.

The scholar was looked upon with favor by the ladies, and his intimate attentions were not unwelcome, for after passing the competitive examinations he could become a government official, and with brains and time, perchance a figure of influence.

Size 8⅜" x 10¼"

REASON FOR VARIATION IN COITAL POSITION

A book or scroll of approximately ten or twelve painted scenes of the intimacies of marriage was given as a wedding gift to the bride and groom, and in some instances by the mother to her daughter, or a mother-in-law to her daughter-in-law The quality of the art varies with the natural implication that the finer work was produced for the wealthier patrons In addition to being a source of instruction, in the older days the pictures were considered to have a protective quality Put into boxes with clothes they supposedly had the charm of warding off moths, worms, and thieves

Gynecologist today are aware that certain coital positions are more conducive to fertility than others It is possible that the learned man of two and three thousand years ago was no less intelligent about the biologic functions than are his present day descendants Thus, in the early bride's books of conjugal instruction and education, variations in posture were suggested together with dates when a woman was most likely to conceive (In light of modern knowledge the calculations were not very accurate)

Pregnancy was important, since a wife's status rose with the birth of a male child who assured the continuation of the family and provided peace for departed ancestors Loyalty of the average Chinese was primarily to his family group and the family system became associated with ancestor worship Ancestor worship is the single most dominating fact in the life of a Chinese

4″ x 7½″ From Brides' Book of 10 Pictures

PAINTING ON SILK

Since the male and female breasts are often drawn identical, the unitiated observer often mistakenly believes both figures to be female The pigtail wrapped about the head, as a variation of male hair styles, further adds to confusion Among the peoples of the world the male skin is darker than the female, as the artist here correctly indicates, thus helping to identify the sexes In a land where thousand died of starvation, the fatty male breasts indicate those who can afford an idealized life of ease, indolence, prosperity and ample food.

People of the world refer to vaginal entrance from the rear as the position of the dog, horse, cat, rabbit, etc , but among the cultured souls of the Celestial Kingdom it was, more subtly, called "The Inverted Flower."

Gynecologists report instances of normally healthy couples whose unions have been barren, in which practice this position has resulted, in many cases, in conception

In a culture which heavily stresses births, especially that of a son, one would not expect to discover much in the way of birth-control techniques This is true, only a very sparse literature exists, and this is devoted to magical procedures and to prescriptions of potions which are as effective as jumping over a broomstick

The features of the girl are quite typical—small mouth, arched eyebrows and very black trim hair adorned with flowers arranged with taste The attitude suggests shyness and reserve, but occasionally when a wisp of hair becomes displaced —and dangles beside her cheek—it is interpreted by the male as wantonness.

BOUND FEET

That different cultures produce widely divergent concepts of physical attractiveness is nowhere better illustrated than in the foot fetishism of China. For many centuries the tiny, bound feet of the upper-class Chinese woman were esteemed as the highest mark of feminine beauty, and admiration and worship of them, evidenced in every art form, represented the most sophisticated expression of the Chinese sensual imagination Poets sometimes likened the bound foot to a "golden lily."

The intense and prolonged suffering which the Chinese girl went through for the sake of achieving this distinctive mark of beauty testifies to the strength of the fetichism it represented. From the age of about six, the toes were wrapped in bindings which were gradually drawn tighter and tighter until the feet became no more than stubs as little as 2½ to 3 inches long. Walking on them was both awkward and uncomfortable, but the mincing tread and undulating motion of the body which they caused were, apparently, exciting to the Chinese male libido.

The erotic attraction of bound feet was reflected in many interesting ways. In some cultures, a lady's handkerchief or some part of her apparel was treasured by her suitor; in China it was the loved one's dainty, embroidered shoe which the adoring lover kept hidden away, carefully wrapped in paper and scented with incense. The gay blade in search of amorous adventure would sometimes drop something intentionally close to a lady's foot, and as he stooped to pick it up he would brush his hand caressingly against her shoe.

In erotic art the female foot is often pictured as being held, caressed or admired by the male. At the same time it is strik-

ing that the feet are never shown bare in any typical Chinese graphic representation. Even when the woman is otherwise completely nude, her feet remain concealed by shoes or some other form of covering.

Bound feet were believed to contribute to a woman's sexual attractiveness in another, more indirect way. The constraint upon the feet, which naturally restricted locomotion, was supposed to fatten the lips of the vulva, which made for greater sexual enjoyment by the male.

UNBOUND FEET

(Private Collection)

Here for the first time we find the female's foot rendered in normal proportion which indicates these sculptured terra cotta figures are of recent vintage, but the age old taboo of the female foot being covered is still rigidly observed.

Just as words are the writer's medium and sound the musician's, so are line and color the medium of the artist. But words, sounds, line and color alone are not enough; those who use them, if they would produce something valuable and enduring, must be fired by a deep emotional feeling or an idea which demands expression. These in turn must be rooted in universal human experience.

It is easy, then, to understand why the union of the sexes has left its indelible mark in the art of every age and every civilization. What human experience is more universal and moving than the act of procreation, what subject more inspiring to the artist—himself a creator—than the wondrous union that begets life itself? To the religious, God is the ultimate creator of all things. What, then, is more godlike than to create?

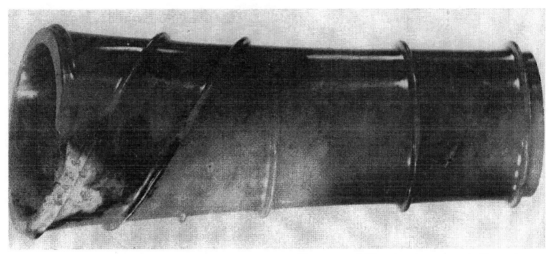

JADE TUBE

Devices designed to increase sexual power and enjoyment are a common form of erotica in many lands. The Chinese jade tube shown here was used as a brace for the penis, serving to keep it rigid for protracted periods of intercourse. The penis was passed through the tube, which was then held in place by the swelling of the protruding extremity. Since jade is chilling to the touch, it is surmised that the instrument was first warmed in some manner before being used.

The primary emphasis in such devices found in China was on heightening the pleasure of the male rather than that of the female. Nevertheless, that feminine satisfaction was not wholly disregarded is indicated by the raised ridges on the outside of the tube, their evident purpose being to provide greater friction against the clitoris and hence greater pleasure for the female partner. Other tubes of this kind are found with perfectly smooth outer surfaces.

The tube shown here dates from the late Eastern Chou Dynasty and is fashioned of brownish green jade. The dimensions are: length, 4¼ inches; diameter at widest point, 1¾ inches; thickness, 3/16 inch. There are some calcinated spots near the rim. Jade stem was a term used for penis in the great classic novel Ching Ping Mei.

FOLDING FAN
Ten Sticks Each 11½ inches

Concealment and disguise are important elements in the erotic art of the Orient, and the folding fan, because its decorated surfaces are hidden from view when the fan is closed, lends itself naturally to this form of art. The fan illustrated here is decorated with three erotic scenes on each side. Its ribs are of highly polished wood, and the guards are inlaid with ivory.

In the Orient the fan is much more than a utilitarian device for keeping cool in the sweltering heat of summer. Oriental philosophers invested it with special symbolic meaning, while in the hands of Japanese and Chinese artists it became a rich medium of a esthetic expression.

The fan is looked upon as a symbol of man's life. The rivet end is the starting point, and the ribs spreading outward from it symbolize the gradual broadening of knowledge and experience as one moves on toward an ever richer future. Because of this special significance, fans are often given as New Year's and wedding gifts, or as a token of good wishes on the occasion of a first meeting with a stranger.

Jade Carving

Here the artist has given enduring expression to the joy of sexual fulfillment in skilfully carved jade, the symbol of constancy and one of the most prized media of Chinese art.

For reasons mysterious to everyone but themselves, the Chinese valued jade as the most previous substance in the world. It is one of the hardest materials to work and only Oriental patience could have shaped it into beautiful works of decorative art. Chinese jade is now valued by wealthy collectors, not for the intrinsic value of the material, but for the fine craftsmanship that shaped it.

71

Paul Segal Collection

Ching Dynasty, Tung Che Period (1862-1875)

PORCELAIN PILLOW

3⅝ inches x 6 inches x 11 inches

What constitutes comfort varies among peoples. The Chinese sit on angular chairs with hard bottoms, lie on hard beds, and rest their heads on hard bricks or porcelain pillows, apparently quite oblivous to any discomfort.

The type of furniture is shown on two sides of this vitrious pillow that is delicately decorated with eight scenes of conjugal intimacies, including one on which the couple share the same bath tub. Body contours are outlined in red and shaded with flesh tones.

These pillows were given to the newly-united couple as a wedding gift in pairs in lieu of instruction books to the young bride.

In the bedroom scenes there are but few articles of furniture, no closets, no cupboards, no bureaus, for the Chinese have infinitely fewer articles of linen or clothing to store than do other peoples.

72

STEEL OPIUM PIPE

Approximately 17 inches Long

Engraved inside the stem of this steel opium pipe are many erotic scenes. None are apparent to the casual observer, until the three rings which hold the stem together are slipped off, permitting the halves where the scenes are concealed to separate.

Opium gives a sense of physical well being. It retards the reactions of the organs of elimination, prolongs erection and lengthens the period of pleasure.

A Courtesan and Her Lover

Cylindrical Pink and White Porcelain Snuff
Bottle painted with touches of green and
purple.

Music is the voice of love and while the
lady plays a transverse flute her lover ac-
companies her with his clappers or castanets.
A sense of ease and tranquility seems to per-
meate most Chinese erotica in contrast to the
rush and aggressiveness of other peoples'.
It implies the idea how long can we make
this last rather than how quickly can we get
thru. In distraction lay the art of prolonging
the act.

According to ancient Confucian teachings
regarding the upbringing of women, it was
considered improper for girls of good family
to learn to play musical instruments or to
study literature or painting, because such
things were thought dangerous to their
morals. But these taboos did not apply to
the courtesan. Alone among Chinese women,
she cultivated learning and the arts so that
men would turn to her for mental diversion
as well as sensual pleasure. The courtesan
thus earned a place among the intelligentsia
of her day and occasionally, through keeping her finger on the pulse of political affairs, came to wield considerable influence.

Glass and Rock Crystal

Snuff Bottles Interior Painting. Flattened
flask with decoration painted in polychrome.

The superlative craftsmanship of the Chinese artist is particularly well demonstrated
in the development of the art of painting
on glass or crystal. The technique used is,
in many ways, more complicated than that
employed in painting on canvas or silk and
requires great imagination, skill and pains-
taking effort.

The artist painting on a cloth surface
generally outlines his figures first, then fills
in the details, and adds the shading last. In
painting on glass, the order is reversed:
shading first, details next, and outlining the
figures last. Moreover, the artist paints on
the opposite side of the glass from that facing the viewer. Once the paint is applied,
no changes are possible.

Erotic pictures done on glass appear at
times on folding panels concealed in a vanity box. The example shown here is a
snuff bottle, which has a scene of love-
making delicately—and dexterously—painted
on the interior surface.

Height 3¼ inches

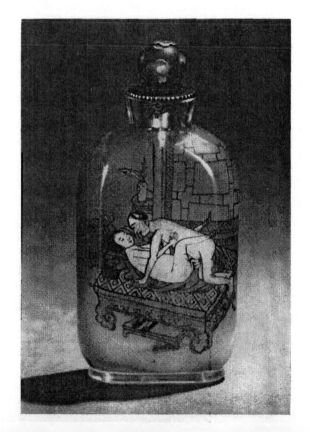

GREEN AND CORAL RED PORCELAIN SNUFF BOTTLE with figures on both sides in relief of men and women sporting in a summer pavillion. Touches of blue and gold.

In the special world of the art collector, there are few objects which hold greater charm and beauty than Chinese snuff bottles. These miniature vase-like containers are small enough to fit comfortably in the palm of the hand, holding only about a tablespoonful of snuff or of medicine. A whole collection of them can be housed in a single small box, yet a collection of infinite variety—with pieces exquisitely carved from jade, amber and agate; glass pieces skillfully blown, pressed and molded, or ingeniously cut, deep-chiseled and undercut; crystalline glass decorated by paintings on the inside surface; and ornately designed pieces of porcelain, ivory and cloisonne. The stoppers, too, are frequently works of art, with a tiny bone or ivory spoon attached to them for use in measuring out the contents. Snuff was taken by emptying a pinch onto the surface of the thumbnail and then inhaling it through the nostrils. The use of snuff became popular and fashionable about 1680. Tobacco was introduced into China in 1530. Prior to this the bottles had long been used as pocket containers for medicine.

WHITE PORCELAIN SNUFF BOTTLE with Brilliant Red and Green Glaze; Ivory Spoon attached to Stopper. Height—2½ inches.

The sundry items illustrated in this study astonish both collectors and dealers, who are ignorant of the existence of such material. Unlike the Japanese, who were frank about sexual matter, the Chinese were extremely secretive.

The photographic evidence here presented, demonstrates that the Chinese, like other human beings, had a very positive interest in such matters. As has been aptly said: "The pendulum of history swings between the vagina and the penis."

The high relief figures of this brightly colored snuff bottle portrays one variant of the theme which illustrates the 'urge of urges'.

In the China of yesterday, no gentleman invited his friends to his home to meet his wife and his daughters. If he wished to show them courtesy, he invited them to a restaurant where, as part of the entertainment, young girls were provided as entertainers.

During the marriage ceremony the officiants called on the spirits of Heaven, of Earth, and of the ancestors to witness the act. During the restaurant ceremonies, as is shown in these somewhat naive representations, the witnesses were more material and tangible.

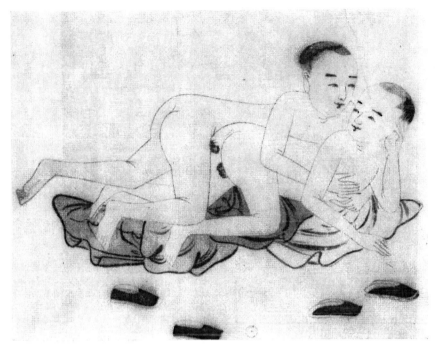

Painting on Silk

HOMOSEXUAL ACTIVITY

It is generally characteristic of most of the races of the world that the male skin is darker than that of the female, a difference that is accurately reflected in the pictorial art of many lands. An interesting variation of this is seen in the painting of two homosexuals illustrated here, the Chinese artist giving the passive pederast a skin lighter in hue than that of the active male partner

Interest centered in anal copulation, active and passive. Oral activity was not common.

In the theater female parts were played by young men trained from youth to skillfully simulate voice, walk and manners. In Tientsin in 1860 there were 35 brothels with 800 boys who were trained for pederastic prostitution. They offered themselves to spectators at evening theatrical performances. Male prostitutes were also found at inns and on canals. Boys trained in the coquetry of the profession appeared at feasts given by rich Chinese.

In those cultures where the male is lord and female virtually a slave homosexuality appears in greater degree. A corollary can be established between homosexuality and the social status of woman, i. e., the higher her status the less male homosexuality.

HAIR AND FEMININE BEAUTY

The Chinese are among the least hirsute of races, and this natural characteristic developed through the centuries into an essential attribute of feminine comeliness. It was prescribed that a girl, to be sexually attractive, must have only to few delicate wisps of pubic hair radiating outward, not unlike the rays of the setting sun. (The frequently recurring parallel between the sun and the organs of reproduction is readily apparent here.) It was also considered essential that the hair itself be as fine and soft as silk, and that none should appear around the anus.

The girl in this painting exemplifies these peculiarly Chinese aesthetic desiderata.

One finds no illustration of older women in the act of love or amorous sporting. Older women do occur but they are in the capacity of servants or shown with derision and for humor in an act of defecation. Young women were considered the only ones worthy of attention since their responses strengthened a man and added years to his life.

Collection of the French Government

77

EMPEROR'S LOVE CART

Chinese legend has it that the Emperor Yang, of the ancient Sui Dynasty (581-618 A.D.), was an assiduous inventor of new devices for heightening the pleasures of sexual indulgence. Here is an artist's conception of one of these purported inventions, a specially constructed horse-drawn cart with wheels that were not perfectly round, imparting a rhythmic lurching motion to the vehicle and its amorous occupants.

Whether this cart represents fact or fancy cannot be determined from references presently at hand. Such a large and frail construction, during the vicissitudes of centuries, could have been destroyed many times but we do have extant evidence of man's effort to heighten his pleasure in the form of a metal pronged device, not unlike our present day safety pin, which was fastened to the base of the penis to constrict the blood and thereby prolong the period of erection.

A silk band wound tightly around the base of the enlarged member are mentioned in erotic novels of the Ming period.

French National Library, Cira 1850

THE SWING

The Chinese are often vulgarly regarded in the West as a staid, austere and stoical people more given to the strict observance of prescribed social formalities than to flights of fancy. Despite this outward austerity, or perhaps as a counterbalance to it, Chinese art is usually rich in creative imagination and originality—qualities which are abundantly evidenced in the particular realm of erotic art and literature.

The painting reproduced here shows a pair of lovers using a swing as a means of sexual divertissement. The art work shows some characteristics which are not typically Chinese, suggesting that the painter may have been a Chinese artist with western training, or possibly an Occidental imitator of Chinese-style painting.

DILDOS

(Left Center Picture)

Male masturbation is rarely, if ever, encountered in Chinese erotic literature or art prior to the Revolution of 1911, probably because of the common belief that it deprived the masturbator of the essence which preserved his health and lengthened his life. On the other hand, a woman was not believed to suffer such consequences, and female masturbation is accordingly an oft-recurring subject of erotica.

Picture paintings frequently illustrate the use by women of objects formed like the male genitalia for purposes of sexual self-satisfaction. These devices are referred to in Chinese as **Kuo Hsien Shing,** or artificial male lotus root or bud. Some pictures show women using them on themselves; in others they are being applied by a second person, sometimes by an old man, sometimes by another female.

For use between two women, as in the painting shown here, the artificial organ is equipped with a cord so that it may be fastened to the waist of the woman filling the male role. There are also pictures of a double device, consisting of two penises fastened together at the scrotum ends, which enabled both partners to gain satisfaction at the same time. However, to what exent such dildos were actually used, or were rather the fanciful creations of male imagination, is still a subject for serious research.

DUALISTIC PRINCIPAL OF NATURE

Pairs play an important part in the life and philosophy of the Chinese.

The symbol at the very start of this book, that of Yang and Yin, illustrates the dual forces of creation. In addition to the human pairing seen in the neighboring picture are balancing pairs of lanterns, of round garden stools and of calligraphic pictures of a poetic couplets.

POSITIONS VARIOUSLY NAMED
(Right Top Picture)

Cultures of the world vary tremendously in the names they give to the different positions of coitus. That seen in the accompanying illustrations is called the "Shrimp" by the Chinese, which is an applicable appellation. This marine crustacean when it appears upon the market place or cooked upon the plate is curled in the form of a "C", which is the shape the human body assumes in this posture.

LOW FURNITURE
(Pictures to right)

The Chinese lived a great deal both outdoors and in garden pavillions. At first they sat on the ground or on mats, later they added tables with elbow rests. They made beautifully simple and magnificently proportioned furniture of hard woods.

The low couches with foot rest lend themselves to erotic activity in which the male plays a passive role, a part not out of keeping with the ideal that a gentleman put forth at all times a minimum of effort. The monumental calm, the unhurried certainty of an old, wise race, shines from all facets of Chinese life—including that of the sexual act

Their love of geometrical design is seen in the zig zag furniture as well as a railing column, cupboard door and window grill.

WOMEN
(Lower Right Picture)

Under the old customs of China, polygamy was an accepted institution, and having a plurality of wives was merely a matter of purse and position. A man was free to take as many as he could afford to support Nor was any strong stigma attached to prostitution, which the Chinese regarded as serving a definite social purpose

It was not the custom for women to be present at banquets The only sign of them on such occasions might be the sound of giggling as they peeped in on the party through a crack between the screens or a slightly opened door. After a feast, however, sing-song girls might be summoned to provide entertainment They would dance and sing, and any guest who felt so inclined might retire with one of them to smoke a pipe of opium and enjoy a bout of lovemaking. There were no bars against bringing such professional entertainers into one's home.

ILLUSTRATED LOVE TALE

Text and Illustration Originally Printed During Wan-Li Reign
Period in 20 Volumes

"Then Golden Lotus asked if he would like to join her, and told the maid to bring the bath water. The tub was set down, the water poured in, and the two got down from the bed to bathe in the fragrant water. They played about as merrily as fishes. When they had spent some time washing themselves, Hsi-men Ch'ing set Golden Lotus on the bathing-board and, holding her feet in his two hands, mounted upon her and thrust forward. They jumped up and down and shook about, two or three thousand times, making a noise like a crab crawling in the mud.

From **The Golden Lotus** (Ching P'ing Mei)

INTRODUCTION TO CHING PING MEI

A Basic Classic Of Major Permanent Value

The classics are those books which cheat death and live beyond their years What fire, worms and decay could not destroy men attempted with censorship, but because other men possessed that intelligence which recognizes merit Ching Ping Mei has lived.

Some say the story which relates to the rise and fall of Hsi Men Ching—husband, lover, business man and government official—is the work of a single hand, Wang Shi-cheng (-1513)   Some believe it is work of many professional story tellers who polished it to flawless perfection during centuries of repetition.

An endless procession of characters pass thru its pages Each is delineated with clarity, individuality and a penetrating understanding of human nature Each slips neatly into his place and the reader does not feel that they clutter the story. All are marvelously alive.

The novel which is set in the reign of Hui Tsung (A D 1101-26), ruthlessly records all Hsi Men Ch'ings dealings justly and unjustly, honestly and dishonestly, in and outside his large household, with his wives, concubines, go-betweens, prostitutes, friends, servants, acquaintances, employees, customers, supervisors, visitors, mendicants, officialdom, etc, etc, etc

In addition to that insight into manners, behavior and character which one expects from a great novel, Ching Ping Mei is delightful entertainment, a rich treasure of information on many subjects, including erotica.

UNDERLYING PHILOSOPHY

Those who wish to give the novel an underlying philosophy say it illustrates the vanity and emptiness of wine, women and wealth gotten at the expense of corruption, using to prove the point a typical family that rose to fortune, flourished, and sank to ruin during a period when Chinese officialdom was exceedingly corrupt

Amid the immense variety in Ching Ping Mei is a fresh kind of humor that depends upon speaking without self consciousness of the body's parts and of their functions The author, unabashed and unafraid, consistently describes life as it is, not as it should be, lived He tells of his characters what they wore, how they looked, what they ate, drank and said

A SCENE OF TIMELESS BURLESQUE

Woodblock Print (1573-1620)

Among the most singular incidents in the World's amorous literature is here illustrated from the great Ming Classic, **Ching P'ing Mei tz' uhua,** in which Hsi-Men Ch'ing, the Chinese Casanova, ties the feet of his taunting fifth wife, Golden Lotus to a trellis in their garden and sitting back with his arm about her maid-servant, sips his wine and using Golden Lotus's frogs' mouth (vagina) as a target leisurely throws plumbs plucked from a handy fruit bowl till one lodges in the innermost flower. (See Chapter on Ching Ping Mei, Page 85.

Each character remains clearly delinated to the end, each in his own way performs the innumerable trivalities of daily life that fill the gaps between birth, marriage and death As the long line of men and women passes by we see them as ordinary people doing the ordinary things eating, drinking, laughing, fighting, gossiping and making love Every passion is represented; every facet of life We establish contact with them through the character of the nouveau riche Hsi Men Ching and his peppery fifth wife, Golden Lotus The story narrates the events of the climatic years of their life

The selections that follow are like fragments of a composition for an entire orchestra played on a single instrument; the sweep of the whole is lost. But if these selections induce the reader to enjoy this classic in its entirety, they will have served their purpose

Abridged and markedly castrated editions have appeared recently in English. To obtain popular circulation, brilliant jackets and alluring illustrations promise the reader the very selections which must be omitted to avoid censorship To correct this misrepresentation for those seriously interested in the literary art, certain of the missing sections are here included Some may find the episodes and escapades translated from the Latin that follow, a handy supplement to the truly masterful translation by Clement Egerton, published by Routledge & Kegan Paul Ltd, London, 1939 and reprinted in 1953 under the title **The Golden Lotus** to which edition volume number and pages refer See page 90.

A UNIQUE SCENE

See Illustration Page 84

"The Plum in the Golden Vases" is another name for Ching Ping Mei. It is a descriptive phrase with which to illustrate a delightful and extremely important point.

Those who enjoy exercise of the mind can find much in the Chinese to charm. The pessimist complains the Chinese never say what they mean. The optimist compliments them as being an astute, sane and happily subtle people.

Lending itself to helpfully unravel this mystery is the first erotic episode in Ching Ping Mei. During a love duet in their spacious gardens, Hsi Men Ch'ing in a mood of playful whimsy pushes his fifth wife, Golden Lotus onto a table, ties her legs to an overhanging arbor, sits back, leisurely sips his wine, picks up a plum from the fruit bowl at hand, aims, and tosses it at her vagina Missing, he tries again until the fruit lodges in its mark

Ask a coldly factual minded person, who desires every word to mean precisely what is said, to give a caption to this episode— ageless in its humor—unique in world literature—and the answer is a blunt, unvarnished crudity, while the cultured soul with cleverly concealed symbolism lifts his description to the realms of poetry.

Example By simply using "vases" as a synonym for vagina the phrase "The Plum in the Gold Vase" takes on a significance that does not disturb the aesthete and gives immense and chuckling pleasure to the scholar who divines its additional implications

Thus the caption of this renowned classic, that has and will survive into the ages, instead of being named "The Plum in the Cunt" will continue to be referred to by those who so choose as "The Plum in the Golden Vase" and once this key, this difference in chosen words is understood, much in Chinese culture, thought, language and way of life stands illuminated

EXCERPTS FROM CHING PING MEI

HSI-MEN CH'ING PLAYS THE GAME OF FLYING ARROWS WITH A LIVING TARGET

See Illustration Page 84

Hsi-men Ch'ing rose and took off his jade-colored light gown. He hung it on the trellis, and went to wash his hands by the peony arbour. When he came back, Golden Lotus had already prepared the mat and its cushions inside the arbour of the vines, and had undressed till not a thread of silk remained upon her body. She lay flat on her back, a pair of crimson shoes still upon her feet, fanning herself with a white silk fan to gain some relief from the heat.

When Hsi-men Ch'ing saw her, his wanton heart was quickly stirred, for the wine had not been without its effect upon him. He took off his clothes, and sat down on a stool, letting his toes play around the treasure of this beautiful flower.

Signs of voluptuousness flowed from her like the juice of a snail which makes a white and sinuous path. Hsi-men took off her ornate red sandals, loosened the ribbons which bound her feet and tied them to the trellis so that she seemed like a Golden Dragon showing its nails. Her entrance gate was revealed and her purple valley disclosed.

Hsi-men Ch'ing lay down and, taking his weapon in his hands, prepared to storm the breach, resting one hand upon the pillow, and proceeding to the attack as he had played "Feathers through the Arch" when at the Flying Arrow game. He strove with all his strength, till from the scene of combat a mist arose, spiralling, like an eel rising from the mud

Golden Lotus beneath him never ceased to murmur, "Darling, my darling" Then, as he was about to reap the fruits of victory, Plum Blossom came suddenly with the wine for which Hsi-men had asked. But when she saw them she put down the jar of wine, and fled to the top of the artificial mound, and there went into the arbour which was called the Land of Clouds She rested her elbows on the chess-table, and amused herself setting out the chessmen Hsi-men Ch'ing lifted his head and looked at her then he beckoned her to come down, but she refused "If you don't come down, I will make you," he cried. He left Golden Lotus and ran up the stone steps to the arbour Plum Blossom fled down a tiny path to the right, through the grottos, till she reached the half-way point, where, among the hanging foliage and flowers, she tried to hide. Hsi-men Ch'ing caught her there, and took her in his arms "I've got you at last, little oily mouth," he cried Then he carried her like a feather to the Arbour of the Vines

"Have a cup of wine," he said, laughing, setting her on his knee, and they drank together mouth to mouth Suddenly Plum Blossom saw that her mistress's feet were tied to the trellis.

"I don't know how you could do such a thing," she said "It is the middle of the day, and if anybody should come in, what would they think of such goings on "

"Isn't the corner gate shut?" Hsi-men asked
"Yes," Plum Blossom said, "I shut it when I came in "

"Now," Hsi-men said, 'watch me. I'm going to play Flying Arrows with a living target. The game is called "Striking the Silver Swan with a Golden Ball. Watch! If I hit the mark at the first shot, I shall treat myself to a cup of wine." He took a plum from the iced bowl, and cast it toward Golden Lotus' gate. Three times he threw and each time the fruit reached the inmost flower. One plum stuck but Hsi-men made no effort to dislodge it or complete the work he had earlier begun. Golden Lotus was languid from exertion and torment Her starry eyes were half closed, and her body fell back limply upon the mat. "You are indeed a roguish enemy," she murmured "You will be the death of me " Her voice trembled.

Composite Picture of Ivory and Semi-Precious Stones

CUNNILINGUS

In cultures where the female has traditionally been subservient to the male, the primary emphasis in sexual relations appears to have been placed on the pleasure and satisfaction of the male, with less regard for the enjoyment of the female. This characteristic is reflected in the erotic art of China, which only rarely pictures the male in a subservient role as in this unusual portrayal of cunnilingus. Where women enjoyed higher status, their sex gratification received correspondingly greater attention, and there are more frequent evidences of this practice.

Hsi-men paid no attention to her, but told Plum Blossom to fan him, while he refreshed himself with wine Then he lay down in an easy chair, and went to sleep.

Hsi-men Ch'ing slept for an hour or so, and when he opened his eyes, Golden Lotus' white legs were still hanging from the trellis Plum Blossom had gone Again his passion was aroused

"Now, you abandoned little creature," he cried, "I'll attend to you." He took out the plum, and gave it to her to eat Then, sitting on the pillow, he took from a pocket in his gown a case of love instruments. First he put on the clasp, and tied a sulphur ring about the root of evil. Not wishing to enter, he lingered long so that Golden Lotus cried furiously "Sweetheart, darling, either be a man quickly or I will go out of my mind I see what it is. You are angry with me. That is why you tease me like this. But now I have found how cunning you can be, I will never make you angry again"

"Ah," said Hsi-men, laughing, "so you have learned your lesson Well, speak nicely to me"

With one blow he penetrated to her marrow and withdrew Then he began looking in his pocket till he found a powder which could summon the pleasure of the marriage bed. He scented his yard and put it into the mouth of the frog. He attacked again. This time the warrior appeared tall and proud, full of fiery ardor Golden Lotus lying on the mat murmured with half closed eyes "O my bearded delight. You do not know what you are putting into me. Your thing arouses me to fury Spare me, I pray" Thus she pleaded shamelessly but Hsi-men without delay attacked with all his strength, putting his hands on the mat, now pulling out, now stabbing to the deepest point a hundred times before again withdrawing. Golden Lotus wiped her wound with a napkin, but in vain The mat clearly indicated the fight and the warrior still unwrinkled and ferocious did not wish to stop

"It is time," exclaimed Hsi-men, "for the monk to strike the gong." With a sudden thrust he reached the citadel, within the woman's gate, which like the stamen of a flower, when touched, is affected with wonderful pleasure. She felt pain and drew herself back while in her body the sulphur ring rattled and broke.

She closed her eyes and her breath came faintly; only a faint murmur issued from her lips, the tip of her tongue became icy cold, and her body fell back apparently lifeless upon the mat

Hsi-men was alarmed. He hastily untied the ribbons, and removed the sulphur ring It was broken into two pieces Then he helped the woman sit up, and at last her starry eyes began to gleam and show life. "Darling," she said in a caressing voice, "you must not do this again. It is not simply fun. My head and eyes swim so that I hardly know where I am."

The sun was already setting Hsi-men hastily helped her into her clothes.

Vol 2 p. 1

Her dainty hands were playing with the warrior between his legs The fellow, who was wearied after the fight and was wearing his silver pin, certainly looked tired but not yet entirely beaten. "Why don't you leave him in peace?" said Hsi-men. "It's your fault You have frightened him so much that he can hardly be moved" "Can hardly be moved!" said she. "What do you mean?" "If he could be," said Hsi-men, "he wouldn't lie like a wilted flower and unable to get up. Why don't you get on your knees and ask forgiveness?" She laughed and looked at him. Then she bent her thigh, put her head on his leg and, seizing the draw-string of his trousers, she caught the warrior in bonds "You are the fellow who was raising his head so high, whose eye was so savage that it scared me. Now you are pretending weariness and are lying as if dead."

Meanwhile she was playing with him, pressing him to her tender cheeks, fondling him with her hand, and finally she kissed the frog's mouth which lay upon her lips. Instantly the warrior was inflamed with anger and arose; his head was (hard as a) finger-nail, his eye was fire, his jaw bristled with hair, his body stands stiff.

Vol. 2 p 97

Hsi-men opened the boy's clothing, took down his party-colored trousers, and gently stroked him

Vol. 2 p 105

He ran his tongue inside the boy's lips, the boy gave a **bellarium suave** and caressed his stiff penis

Vol. 2 p. 147

The weapon seemed wonderful to her, for the veins were swollen with red blood and the flesh was solid and strong . . . (p 148) Finally he bade the woman lie on the bed and having placed her legs around his body with both hands he fiercely threw himself into the battle.

Vol 2 p 149

Porphyry liked one sport above all others Erotically joined to the man, she wanted him to pluck her flower in the rear, and herself to try the innermost flower. Thus satiated she fell into the ecstacy for which lovers strive, and she was so fond of this game that Han Tao-kuo found pleasure in the first gate hardly three times in thirty days Besides, she used to tickle the ivory sceptre with her lips, and fondled it all night, ever unsatisfied If the master wearied, her lips made him strong

Vol 2 p 157

She raised her legs in such fashion that the chicken's tongue appeared Hsi-men asked her to insert the medicament while he himself attached the silver clasp to the base of his penis, added the sulphur ring, and smeared his umbilicus with ointment Then she took his treasure in her hand and wholly united herself to him and enjoyed an almost unceasing embrace Porphyry said, "You'll hurt your legs, won't you? Take the pillow and I shall move my body." And again, "I'm afraid you won't be comfortable. Wouldn't you like me to raise my legs higher-" Hsi-men tied her leg to the bed with a tape, and leaning upon her he served her Unceasingly the fluid of love flowed from her, like a liquid brewed in a spoon Something white also came out, and Hsi-men asked "Why, is this all you have?" He was on the point of clearing himself, but Porphyry said, "No, I'll clear you in my own way," and falling to her knees she cleared him with her clucking tongue

Then Hsi-men, again ablaze with passion, turned her over and tried her flower in the back door But enough sulphur stuck to his penis so that he could hardly make way and was not able to go forward, while she contracted her forehead in pain Hsi-men advanced slowly and Porphyry, by feeling with her hand, discovered that he had completed only half the distance. Set on his body, she turned her head and invited him with her face "Darling," said she, "please go in slowly Your root is too large for me to bear." Hsi-men raised her legs so as to see the motions of his advances and retreats

Vol. 2 p. 158

. . to receive the river of life Hsi-men was so happy that the liquid seemed like a flowing torrent. Then he withdrew himself, still wearing the ring; Porphyry cleared him with her lips.

Vol. 2 p 213

. took his penis in hand and tried her flower in the back-door He pulled himself up and down more than a hundred times, with loud noise

Vol 2 p 315

. I would like to do business with your back-door. He came forward and set the boy in a chair and was kissing him But the boy broke free.

Vol 2 p 317

First he placed the silver clasp at the base of his penis, and attached the sulphur ring above it. Then he took a little of the red powder from the silver box—not more than was prescribed—and placed it in the horse's eye. His penis stood straight—an amazingly terrible sight; its head swelled and the one-eye opened wide, the crosswise muscles were easily visible; it was a yellow color like the liver, nearly seven inches long and much thicker than usual . . The woman, sitting nude upon his lap, took his penis in her hands . He wanted to move his penis forward to its duty, but the head was so swollen that it was a long time before he succeeded, and even then he got only a short distance. At last the woman's fluids of love were flowing and the way began to be easier His penis advanced, but hardly beyond the head. Then the wine which he had drunk came to the rescue His penis, at first gently drawn away, was plunged into the depth and gave him a joy hardly expressible. The woman also arrived at the peak of pleasure; she was lying on the bed as though unable to move and was saying in a choking voice, "My dearest man, your wonderful penis will be the death of me" Soon she whispered again, "My life, my joy, wouldn't you like to pluck love's fruit at the back-door." He turned the woman onto her stomach and advanced his penis again. His attack was so violent as to produce a loud noise "Push in, push in, my darling," cried Porphyry "Don't hold back. If you like, bring the light and your pleasure will be the greater" When the lamp had been moved closer, she spread her legs wide as she lay underneath Hsi-men pulled her apart and rushed in while the woman, for her part, raised her legs to meet him and whispering tremulously massaged the middle of her own flower.

Vol 2 p. 322

. . If a woman's blood touches a man at a time like this is brings bad luck .

The woman raised herself on hands and legs He plunged in, and by the lamp-light marvelled how white her legs were. He propped himself on his hands so as to have the pleasure of seeing the motions of his penis Now he had stretched half-way in, but he could not proceed farther the woman was afraid that the blood would run and she was using a towel to staunch the stream Hsi-men worked for an hour, and finally he pulled her legs apart and forced so complete an entrance that the hair of each tickled the other with no space left between them He felt unbelievable pleasure, but she said, "Please go carefully; what you are doing hurts me " "Now you will have all of me," he said There was a cold drink on the table, and when he had tasted it his semen flowed like water

Vol 2 p 336

and see if your lips can make that fellow collapse, if you can, I'll give you a tael of silver " "I'm ashamed of you, you rascal," said she "How is it going to collapse, seeing that you have drunk that potion?" However, she lay back on the bed and took his penis between her red lips. "It's so enormous that it hurts my mouth " Then she sucked, and tickled the head of his penis with her tongue, and was licking the skin outside and rolling it up and down between her lips. But though she was stroking the giant with her cheeks and was playing in the thousand ways of love, the thing only became longer and thicker. Hsi-men looked at her Her lovely body gleamed inside the silken curtains With smooth hands she took the hairy monster, inserted it between her lips, entirely devoured it, and ejected it in languid state from her mouth

Vol 2 p 337

even if I suck all day, I won't get anywhere at all   .
    . Lying back on the bed, he arranged that she be pulled on top of him "Let me arrange myself first," she said "When I have done that, maybe you will be able to get in " But the head of his penis was so broad that much work on both sides was necessary before the smallest part finally got in The woman, pulled above the man, moved herself one way and the other and could not conceal her pain "My darling," she cried, "that thing hurts me so much that I can't stand it any longer," and feeling herself with anxious hand she discovered that his penis was hardly half inside Gathering some spittle from her mouth, she moistened the inside of her queynt so that the passage was easier. Then she moved herself back and forth and penis gradually went all the way into her vulva

A Scene from a series of 12 paintings on silk dealing with Homosexuality.

LESBIAN ACTIVITY

In the picturesque language of the Chinese mirror grinding is the term used to describe Lesbian activity. The mirror is a flat surface and two flat surfaces rubbed together without stem, protuberance or dominant member conveys the idea of contact of female genitalia with female genitalia.

Among erotic paintings are pictures which show females handling objects resembling in shape the male member. Although on rare occasions such dildoes may have been used for vaginal insertions, to satisfy curiosity, it is believed today they were more of a male, than a female concept, and were little used, if at all.

Had they produced extensive pleasure, it is believed, they would be found in greater numbers than they are.

Vol. 2 p. 338

She leaped (like a male animal), moved forward, emitted a terrifying sound Then they changed places. He held her legs and thrust his penis with all his strength As he strove hard he looked down at her, but he had only slight sensation, and she was simply not becoming fluid With places again changed, the woman embraced his shoulders with her arms and threw herself upon him, inserted her tongue into his mouth, and took his whole penis inside Then she smiled gently—"My darling, either you will finish or I shall die" Soon she became languid; her tongue was cold almost to freezing; the juices of love poured from the woman Hsi-men felt her queynt to be hot, his own liver became hot and was thrilled beyond measure. The juices flowed like a river, so that the woman wiped them away with a towel. Then they exchanged embraces and mutual kisses, but his penis remained stiff . . For an hour they slept, but after sleeping the woman, who was not yet satisfied, raised herself above the man and sported again Again the juices flowed down and at length she began to be exhausted "If it doesn't collapse, come back to me tonight, and my lips will make it subside."

Vol 2 p 348

He bade the woman get on the bed, to raise herself on her hands and feet and to raise her buttocks high. He put some spittle on his penis and moved forward gradually But the head of his member, haughty and unyielding, was willing to go in only a short distance The woman contracted her brows and bit her handkerchief "My darling," said she, "do not go in too fast; my back door is not like the front door I feel you inside as though I were afire"

Vol. p. 349

He held her legs while he watched his penis moving up and down, and cried, "Do me a kindness, you little whore, and call me your darling; then you will take me entirely . . "
He compressed his legs and thrust forward with such an awesome sound that the woman said she could bear no more When the time came, he pulled her backward toward himself, he plunged into the depths of her hollow, he experienced the greatest pleasure With difficulty did he put himself into the woman, she took him entirely; and they lay mingled on the bed. When his penis was withdrawn, it appeared bloody and from its mouth a certain fluid was oozing, which the woman wiped away with a handkerchief, and both of them slept together.

Size 9⅝" x 9⅝"

HOMOSEXUAL PLAY

Female masturbation and lesbian activity occurs with frequency in art representation. It was accepted in life with ready tolerance since the female "essence" was considered limitless in quantity.

However a single male masturbating occurs with extreme rarity, if found at all, for it was believed semen was precious, limited in quantity, and ejaculation resulted in loss of vitality. In male homosexuality there was an exchange of "essence" and thus no loss occurred. The feminine features of these figures are worthy of note.

.   and pushed himself forward with all his strength.   At the first thrust he entered, for the woman, who had long been fondled, was already wet and presented no obstacle at all

Hsi-men and Moonbeam

Vol 3 page 76

Having sent his servant ahead with presents of silver and a light dress, Hsi-men got into his sedan chair and went to visit Moonbeam, the daughter of an old procuress.   In Moonbeam's room the hangings, curtains and bedclothes were all of silk It was a most attractive room and exquisitely perfumed.   "Indeed", Hsi-men said, "this is a dwelling-place for the Immortals to which no mortal man should come "

They talked, laughed, ate mincemeat, played dominoes, drank wine   Moonbeam played a lute and sang   "Love is in our hearts " From exquisite lips came exquisite melody   They cast dice.

Hsi-men took from his sleeve a white silk kerchief in which was wrapped a tiny gold box   Moonbeam thought there were fragrant tea-leaves in it and was going to open it, but Hsi-men said   "That is not for tea-leaves, it holds my medicine "

He took the wine-cup and drank wine with his medicine.   He put his arms around Moonbeam and they drank mouth to mouth   He stroked her breasts   They were small and very soft.   He pulled aside her shift.   Beneath it her skin was as clear as the whitest jade   His passion was aroused and his penis promptly had an erection   Pulling down his trousers, he told Moonbeam to place her hand on his penis, but it was so large that she became afraid.   She threw her arms around Hsi-men's neck and said   "My sweet, we are coming together tonight for the first time   Have pity on me and give me only half.   If you put it all in you will cause me great pain   Your medicine has made it red, warm and so terrifying

Hsi-men laughed and said "Get down, girl, so you can know what this tastes like " "Another time I will do that for you," Moonbean said, "for we shall meet as often as there are leaves upon the trees, but not today, the first time we have come together."

Hsi-men was anxious to begin.   Moonbeam asked if he would not have more wine.   "It is not wine I want," he said, "but to lie with you."

Moonbeam summoned the maid to clear away the wine table and take off Hsi-men's boots. Meanwhile she went to the inner court to take off her clothes and wash herself When the maid had taken off his boots Hsi-men gave her a piece of silver, then he got into bed and she lighted some incense. Moonbeam came back and asked if he would like some tea. "It is not tea I want," he said. Then she fastened the door and pulled down the curtains, put the pillow on the bed and joined him there. They were like a pair of love-birds or the phoenix and his mate

Hsi-men saw that the girl's skin was smooth and fine, and her queynt dainty and without a hair upon it. It was like a piece of pastry made of the finest flour, tender and delicate and perfectly adorable He clasped her waist with both his arms It was as smooth as jade and fragrance issued from it. Not for a thousand gold pieces could such perfection have been bought. He held her white thighs about him, put the clasp in place and pushed himself into the middle of the delightful flower But his penis was so solid that it could not penetrate. He labored for a long time, but did not succeed very well. Moonbeam raised her brows in pain, clutched the pillow and begged him to go easy. But Hsi-men thrust all the more fiercely.

They sported together until the third night-watch. Then Hsi-men Ch'ing went home

HSI-MEN BURNS PORPHYRY

Vol 3 Page 103

A servant boy hearing noise in the room next to where he is sleeping makes a hole in the paper wall and peeping through observes—

The candles were shining brightly. He was surprised to see Hsi-men Ch'ing sporting vigorously with his master's wife, whose legs were plainly to be seen over the frame of the bed. Hsi-men Ch'ing was wearing a short silken vest and nothing at all upon the lower part of his body. At the edge of the bed, he was coming and going, plunging and prancing, making a considerable noise. The woman was saying all kinds of endearments to him Hu Hsiu heard "My darling, if you would like to burn your naughty sweetheart, do so. Burn me whenever and wherever you like I shall not forbid you. My body is all yours, and whatever you like to do with it, you may do."

Hsi-men Ch'ing and Porphyry enjoyed the pleasures of love for a long time   He burned her in three places, at the pit of the stomach, on the mount of Venus, and on the tail bone. Then she got up, dressed herself, and called her maid to bring water that she might wash her hands   Fresh wine was heated; food brought, and they talked together.   After drinking a few cups of wine, Hsi-men Ch'ing mounted his horse and went away.

Hsi-men and Golden Lotus

Vol 3 Page 106

Hsi-men Ch'ing undressed and sat down on the bed.   Golden Lotus stretched out her arm and pulled down his trousers.   She touched his staff.   It was soft.   The clasp was still about it.

"Oh, you dried duck, boiled in a cauldron!" she cried   "Your body may be exhausted, but your mouth is never so.   Look at this gentleman!   Not a word to say for himself!   Now, you villain.   How dare you play tricks with that strumpet Porphyry all this time?   See the state you've brought him to!

Hsi-men Ch'ing laughed.   He could not think of anything to say.   He got ready for bed and told Plum Blossom to heat some wine   Then he took a pill from the little gold box, swallowed it and lay down on the bed.

"My dear," he said, "taste it   If you bring it to life again, good for you."

Golden Lotus swore she would do nothing of the sort.   "You filthy creature!   And it has just been busy in that dirty strumpet's mill   If I did a thing as foul as that, it would kill me."

"You funny little whore," Hsi-men said, "don't talk nonsense.   I tell you I have had nothing to do with her."

"If you have not, why won't you take an oath?"

The argument continued for some time   Finally she invited Hsi-men to wash   He would not.   She took a handkerchief from under the pillow and wiped off his penis, which she took between her red lips in such a way that he soon grew passionate again   Hsi-men mounted her in an impetuous manner, pushed himself forward and while he pressed her thighs with his arms, pushed in his penis with a wonderful sound.

The lamp was shining and he rejoiced at the sight.   Golden Lotus rose in bed to meet his thrusts and kindled even greater desire   He put some red powder on his penis and inserted it again, holding her around the thighs he assaulted her many times.

"Darling," she whispered, "you must do no more. You should not have put the powder on him."

"Now, little strumpet," Hsi-men Ch'ing cried, "are you afraid of me or not? Will you ever treat me disrespectfully again?"

"Darling, forgive me," Golden Lotus said "I will never dare talk like that again Don't thrust so roughly, you will make my hair untidy"

They played happily far into the night, till at last they were tired and went to sleep

Hsi-men and Heart's Delight

Vol 3 Page 340

Hsi-men sat down on a chair and Welcome Spring brought him tea He told her to help him undress Heart's Delight, finding that he was going to spend the night, quickly made the bed and warmed it with a hot-water bottle Then she helped him to bed and Hibiscus went out to shut the corner door. The two maids went to sleep in the other room.

When he asked for more tea, the maids were too sleepy to wish to get it They told Heart's Delight to hurry. She took off her clothes and got into bed with him. The wine he had drunk had aroused Hsi-men's passions. He took a considerable amount of the secret medicine and placed the clasp on his penis Turning the woman on her back, he spread her legs apart and pushed himself fiercely Her tongue grew cold and her vagina ran with moisture like a fountain She called him all the tender names she could think of It was the middle of the night and so silent that the noise they made might have been heard far away Hsi-men Ch'ing found the woman's body as yielding as down He put his arms round her and kissed her, then told her to squat upon the bed and suck him. She did so, to his great satisfaction.

"My Child," Hsi-men said to her, "your skin is as white as the Sixth Lady's was Being with you is like being with her. Treat me well and faithfully and I will be kind to you."

"You must not say that," Heart's Delight said. "Comparing me with her is like comparing Earth with Heaven. But my husband is dead, and, if you do not hate a creature so ugly as I am, look at me sometimes and I shall be more than content."

Hsi-men asked how old she was

"My animal is the Hare, and I am thirty-one."

100

"You are a year younger than I am," he said   He was delighted to find that not only did she talk sensibly, but she was no mean performer on the bed.   Next morning she waited upon him hand and foot, put on his shoes and socks, and helped him to dress his hair.   The two maids, Welcome Spring and Hibiscus, could not get near him.

Hsi-men and Moonbeam
Vol 3 Page 245

Leaving the party they slipped into another room and began to sport upon the bed.   It was piled deep with coverlets   "Won't you take off your clothes, Father?"   Moonbeam asked.

"I am afraid I must keep my clothes on," Hsi-men Ch'ing said   "They will be out of patience waiting for us "   He pulled up the pillow for her.   She took down her trousers and stretched herself upon her back   Hsi-men lifted her dainty feet over his shoulders, then unloosed his blue silk trousers and placed the clasp on his penis.   The heart of the flower lay sweetly folded before him; the tender willow-like waist quivered

> This is a flower so delicate
> It cannot endure violence.
> The wind of spring blows over it unceasingly
> And when it reaches the flower's heart
> Still seems unsatisfied.
> There are no limits to their love.
> Softly she calls him her precious body.
> There are no words can tell
> The happiness of this night of Spring.

For a long time their love followed its course to their great delight.   Hsi-men breathed heavily, and she made strange little noises without ceasing, her hair spread out over the pillow. "My love," she murmured, "do not be so furious "   Then their satisfaction reached its height and semen flowed from him like a river.   The rain ceased and the clouds dispersed   They rose, dressed themselves, and washed their hands.   Then hand in hand, they went back to the hall.

Hsi-men and Golden Lotus
A Scatalogical Experience and Philosophical Commentary
Vol 3 Page 313

Golden Lotus had taken particular pains to make herself look pretty and she had washed her body with perfumed water.

Painting on Paper 6½" x 8⅜" of a series of 12

A Philosopher's Ease

Many a scene of copulation is illustrated in an outdoor setting amid flowers, a rockery and trees. Holding tightly to the bows of a willow this girl moves up and down with the support of the swaying branches while the supine philosopher smilingly takes his ease.

The Chinese in their psychological reaction to things have a profound distrust of logic and are incapable of scientific reasoning. Though they are worshipers of reality and common sense, they are extremely suspicious of arguments that are too perfect. Once they get hold of an idea they keep a tight unrelaxing grip on what they believe to be the truth.

Among these is the belief that intercourse restores strength, that the male acquires the energy of his partner, and the younger the girl the greater the benefits to the man. Thus the older a man gets the younger he desires the woman.

The Chinese have a knack of leaving out the unessentials and grappling the essentials of life, but with his amours he is very specific in specifying sparse, thin, silky pubic hairs, even none at all, as a esteemed sign of desirability, an abundance on the mons venaris is considered an abhorrence.

102

She expected him and, when he came, she smiled sweetly. She took his clothes and told Plum Blossom to make tea. They went to bed, and, under the coverlets, embraced and pressed their tender bodies closely together. She used every one of her hundred charms to give him pleasure. They enjoyed each other for a while, then Hsi-men Ch'ing found that he could not sleep He told her how he had longed for her while he was away. Then, as he was still unsatisfied, he asked her to play the flute for him. She was ready to do anything he asked, so that she might the more firmly establish her hold over him. They had been separated for a long time. She had been starved for love so long that passion set her afire. She would have made herself a part of him. Grasping Hsi-men's penis she wished she could suck it the whole night. Hsi-men wanted to urinate, but Golden Lotus would not let him go away "My charmer" she said, "my mouth will take any amount of your urine. It is chilly tonight and you might take cold if you get out of bed. It would be more trouble."

Hsi-men was delighted "Dearest," he said, "I don't believe anyone else would love me as you do" He urinated into her mouth and visibly she drank it "Do you like it," Hsi-men asked? "It is a little sour," she answered "Give me some fragrant tea-leaves to take the taste away."

"The tea-leaves are in my white silk coat," Hsi-men said, "get them for yourself." Golden Lotus pulled the coat to her, took the tea-leaves, and put them into her mouth.

Readers, concubines are always ready to lead their husbands on and to bewitch them. To this end, they will go to any length of shamelessness and endure any shameful thing. Such practices would be abhorrent to a real wife who had married her husband in the proper way.

Hsi-men Ch'ing and Golden Lotus enjoyed ecstasies of pleasure that night.

Hsi-men and Golden Lotus copulate during an Argument

Vol 3 Page 318

"Little oil mouth," Hsi-men said, "I have several wives, but, as everyone knows, I love you best."

"No, you are deceiving me," Golden Lotus said. "Do you remember how you and Lai Wang's wife were as close together as honey and oil mingled? You never thought about me then. The Lady of the Vase had a baby, and you treated me like a black-eyed hen. You have been secretly carrying on with Heart's Delight. You are such a liar, I don't believe you."

Hsi-men pulled her to him and kissed her "You funny little strumpet," he said "Where did you get such-shaped ears?"

He told her to turn over, and he inserted his penis from behind. Holding Golden Lotus' legs tightly he pushed in noisily. "Do you fear me or not?" he cried "Will you try to control my actions any more?"

"If I didn't," Golden Lotus said, "you would fly off in the air. I know you can't give the woman up, but, if you wish to have her, you must ask my permission "

Hsi-men laughed It was the third night watch before they were content to put their arms around one another and go to sleep They slept till nearly dawn.

Before it was light, Golden Lotus, still hungry for more, fondled his weapon with her slender fingers till it was ready once more for action

"Darling," she said, "I want to lie on you " She climbed on to him, and played the game of making a candle upside down She put her arms about his neck and wriggled about She asked him to grip her firmly by the waist. Then she lifted herself up and dropped herself again soon the penis was completely concealed and the only part that remained outside the vagina was that which was held by the clasp

"Darling," she said, "I will make a red silk belt for you, and you can keep in it the medicine the monk gave you. And I will make two supports which you can tie at the root of your penis and fasten round your waist. When they are tightly tied, it will be soft and your whole penis wil go in all the way. Don't you think this will be better than the clasp which is so hard and troublesome?"

"Yes, my child, make it by all means The medicine is in my little box Put it in for yourself."

"Come back tonight," Golden Lotus said, "and we will see what it is like."

Hsi-men tries Golden Lotus' Belt

Vol. 3 Page 340

Then Golden Lotus went to the chamber and made water. She asked Plum Blossom to get a tub of water so that she could wash. Then she asked what the time was.

"I have been asleep some time," the maid said, "it must be about the third night-watch."

Golden Lotus took down her hair, and went to the inner room The lamp was nearly out. She pulled up the wick. Then dressed and lay down beside him. After a while, she

104

began to toy with his weapon. But Hsi-men had been playing with Plum Blossom, she was not able to get him erect because he was so soft. The wine was inflaming her and sitting on her heels on the bed she put his penis into her mouth. She tickled the opening, she moved the head here and there, and sucked in and out continuously. Hsi-men woke up.

"Now, you funny little strumpet, where have you been all this time?"

We were drinking in the inner court," Golden Lotus said. "The Third Lady gave us a feast and Miss Yu sang. We guessed fingers, threw dice, and played for a long time. I beat Picture of Grace, but Tower of Jade beat me. I had to drink a few cups of wine. Lucky for you that you got away and came here to sleep in peace, but don't think I will let you escape."

"Have you made the belt of ribbon?" Hsi-men said.

"Yes, it is here." She took it from underneath the bed-clothes, showed it to him, then tied it about his prick and around his waist. She tied it very tightly.

"Have you taken anything?" she asked him.

He told her that he had, and she continued her attentions, but she was unable to get the penis erect because it was so soft. The wine was inflaming her and sitting on her heels she put his penis into her mouth. She tickled the opening, moved the head here and there, and sucked continuously.

She continued her attentions while the penis grew stiff, with vigor and arose straight up, longer than usual. She was lying on Hsi-men, but his penis was so large that she had to stretch her vagina with both hands before it could enter her. When at last he had entered, grasping his neck with her hands, she asked Hsi-men to hold her waist and slowly pressing, the penis went all the way in.

"My delight," she said, "put the silk vest under you."

Hsi-men folded the red belt twice and placed it under his loins. Then Golden Lotus moved again and swallowed up his penis.

"Sweetheart," she said, "It has gone in all the way. It has filled me entirely. Do you like it?"

Hsi-men putting his hand down there knew that the penis had gone in so far that no space remained, not even enough for a hair. Only the testicles remained outside and he enjoyed the utmost pleasure.

"I am cold," said Golden Lotus, "let us move the lamp. It was more pleasant in summer Don't you think this ribbon is better than the clasp? It does not pain me, it makes your prick longer. If you don't believe me, place your hand over my belly. I feel that it reaches my marrow. Embrace me and let me sleep on top of you."

"Sleep, girl" said Hsi-men, "I will hold you"

She inserted her tongue into his mouth, closed her eyes, and placing her arms around him, slept. Nevertheless, love soon excited her. She pressed his shoulders, sat up straight, and leaped up and down so rapidly that his penis went all the way each turn. "I am dying", my sweetheart," she cried They enjoyed each other moving with opposing strokes and Hsi-men withdrew first from the fight.

"Embrace me" said Golden Lotus, and gave him her breasts to suck. Then she languished and the love fluid flowed out of her The neck of her womb seemed to leap within her. She relaxed her arms and thighs and covered herself with her hair. Nevertheless, the penis having been withdrawn still remained stiff and Golden Lotus wiped it off with a napkin

"What shall we do, darling? It is not enough for you even yet."

"Let us go to sleep now," Hsi-men said. "We will settle that question afterwards."

"I feel as though I were paralyzed," Golden Lotus said.

"So the mystery of clouds and rain was performed once more. They lay down to sleep and did not wake again till dawn.

At dawn, Golden Lotus and Hsi-men awoke Golden Lotus saw that his weapon was still upright like a ramrod. "Darling", she said, "you must forgive me, but I can stand no more I will suck your penis."

"Suck it", said Hsi-men, "if you can soften it, it will be well."

Golden Lotus sitting on her haunches put her hands on his legs and took the penis into her mouth She sucked for a whole hour but it did not languish. Hsi-men placing his hands on her white neck now moved in, now drew out his penis from her lips with all his force. Soon the lips were wet with white spume (and made the penis red with their own color.)

"I have a favor to ask of you," Golden Lotus said. "I wonder whether you will grant it me."

"What is it, you little strumpet?"

"Will you give me the Sixth Lady's fur coat?

"You little strumpet, you never lose a chance of doing well for yourself. That fur coat is worth at least sixty taels of silver."

She rubbed the penis softly against her cheeks and put it in her mouth. She tickled the opening and her tongue excited the nerve. She held it firmly with her lips and moved gently. Hsi-men was delighted and with growing pleasure prepared to yield. Holding it firmly, she cried "let the semen flow", and she sucked as it went into her mouth. Hsi-men dressed and went out. Golden Lotus stayed in bed.

"Bring me the coat now," she said. "If you put it off you will be too busy."

Vol 3 Page 357

Hsi-men and Heart's Delight, his deceased Sixth Wife's Servant

When there was no one else in the room Hsi-men made Heart's Delight sit on his knee and they drank wine from mouth to mouth. He unfastened her dress and uncovered her tender white bosom. He touched her nipples. "My child," he said, "I know nothing so sweet as your lovely white skin. It is as beautiful as your lady's and, when I hold you in my arms, I feel as if I held her."

Hsi-men drank more wine. Then Heart's Delight cleared everything away and gave him some tea. She found fresh silken bed-clothes, and an embroidered pillow. She warmed them and asked him whether he would rather sleep on the large bed or the small one. "I prefer the small one," he said. Heart's Delight put the bed-clothes on the small bed and helped him to undress. She went to the other room to wash, came back, and fastened the door. When she had put the lamp beside the bed, she undressed and got into bed with him.

The woman touched the warrior. The clasp was already in position. It was very hard and frisky and she felt pleased and terrified at the same time. They kissed each other and set to. Hsi-men, seeing her lying on the bed without any clothes on, was afraid she might catch cold. He picked up her vest and covered her breast with it. Then he took her by the legs and thrust forward violently. Heart's Delight gasped for breath and her face became very red.

"Mother gave me that vest," she said.

"My dear," said Hsi-men, "never mind about that. Tomorrow, I will give you half a roll of red silk to make underwear, and you shall wear it when you wait on me."

"Thank you," Heart's Delight said.

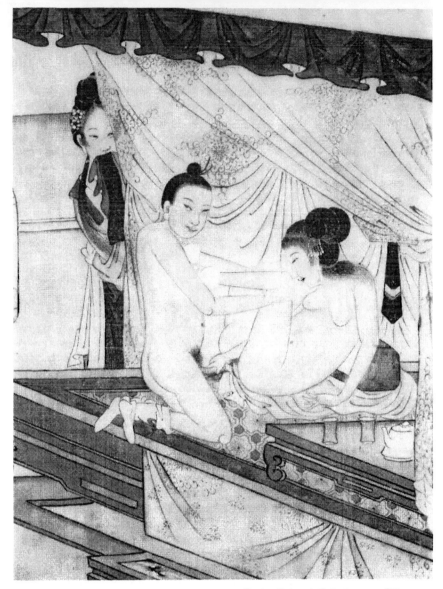

Gayly Colored Painting on Silk

PEEPING

While there are those cultures which seek utmost seclusion for the intimacies of the sexual embrace, there are those, among them the Chinese, that do not seem to be abashed by the presences of a third person or more.

In life there are those, predominantly males, who are aroused by observing others, and those who likewise are stimulated by knowing they are being watched.

In Chinese erotic art and literature peeping plays no minor role. Confined to the home, as the women were, they clung to any bit of divertissement that chance might offer, thus sneaking to and away from curtained doors and latticed windows to eavesdrop became a household skill.

103

"I have forgotten how old you are," Hsi-men said

"I am thirty-two years old"

"A year older than I am," he said

They went on with their love-making, and he called her Chang IV "My daughter," he said, "serve me well, and when the Great Lady's baby is born, you shall have charge of it And, if you yourself bear a son to me, I will make you one of my ladies and you shall take the dead lady's place."

"My husband is dead, and I have no relatives of my own," Heart's Delight said "I have no other wish than to serve you, and I never want to leave you If you take pity on me I shall always be grateful."

Hsi-men was very pleased with the way she spoke He grasped her white legs firmly and plunged forward violently again She murmured softly and her starry eyes grew dim Soon Hsi-men told Heart's Delight to recline with her legs spread like a mare and he rode on her covered with a red coverlet. He forced his penis, and with the light shining, he fondled her white haunches. "Call me your sweetheart," she said," and do not stop Give me the whole length." She raised her pussy to take Hsi-men and called him her delight with a trembling voice They played for a whole hour before Hsi-men was willing to stop At length Heart's Delight took out the penis and wiped it with a napkin. They slept in each others embrace Before daylight excited Heart's Delight took his penis into her mouth.

"Your fifth mother," said Hsi-men, "would suck all night She would not let me go out of bed if I wanted to urinate because she was afraid I would get cold and so she would absorb my liquid"

"What are you referring to," said the girl, "I want to drink too," and Hsi-men urinated into her mouth They made love in every possible way.

The next day, she rose first, opened the door and lighted a fire. Then she helped Hsi-men to dress. He left and went to the front court.

Vol 4 Page 25

Sobbingly the boy Hua T'ung confesses the fondness of Scholar Wen for "hole-and-corner work".

He always comes, said the boy, and wants to make me suffer. He pushed his penis between my buttocks so violently that today they are swollen with great pain When I ask him to stop, he pushes his penis in and out all the more.

Hsi-men Ch'ing makes love to Moonbeam, a singing girl.

With tender fingers she opened his trousers, took out his penis and stroked it caressingly, until it grew rigid and a superb purple color. The man asked her to suck it, she bent her neck, opened her red lips, and received half the penis in her mouth, which she moved here and there with a pleasant noise.

Vol 4 Page 42

Hsi-men Ch'ing pays respects to Mistress Pen who uses cinnamon for powder

He kissed her and put his arms around her. Then, removing the pillow, he placed her on the bed, put her legs over his shoulders, and began to work for the clasp was ready. There was not a long delay before the love juices of the woman flowed so freely that they wet his trousers. Hsi-men drew out his penis, took powder from the chest, put it on the head, and again advanced for the assault. The powder curbed the fluid and the matter was made more confortable. The woman accepted his penis in her anus and spoke very pleasant words Hsi-men, incited by the wine which he had been drinking, held her legs tightly and pushed himself violently. Proceeding with greatest force he entered her almost 300 times, while the woman's hair hung around her shoulders and her tongue was so cold that she could not speak Hsi-men was hardly breathing but suddenly the semen flowed out and he enjoyed the greatest pleasure. After a long rest when he withdrew his penis the love juice flowed out, but the woman wiped it with a napkin. They put on their clothes and the woman dried her cheeks with cinnamon.

Vol 4 Page 49

Hsi-men Ch'ing visits Mistress Pen IV

His lust for the woman was great She opened her legs, opened her cunt with both hands and let the man invade her to the furthest recess. Warm liquid flowed out from her and wet his clothes. On the head of his penis Hsi-men Ch'ing placed considerable powder and then holding fast with both hands, he thrust so vigorously that he went in all the way, not leaving the least part outside.

Vol 4 Page 50

Haughtily he wished to wipe his penis on his trousers but the woman interrupted and said, "I do not want you to wipe it, I will suck it for you." Hsi-men wishing nothing sweeter, she bent over, took the penis in both hands and sucked it until it was clean. Then he put it back in his trousers.

Vol 4 Page 54

Hsi-men visits Lady Lin and after sprinkling the ancient incense myrrh upon her body lights it. The 11th Edition of the Encyclopedia Britanica speaks of the Chinese using myrrh for sexual purposes, but does not explain how. In the following lies an answer.

Vol 4 Page 55

. . . put forth his strong penis in front of her cunt, then he raised himself and he went in with a crash. Hsi-men lit seeds of myrrh upon the belly and the openings to the cunt

Vol 4 Page 58

Ssi-men Ch'ing visits Heart's Delight who gives him milk for his medicine and during intercourse he vents that strong, strange desire of some males to inflict pain upon their mates.

He remembered a considerable quantity of long lasting medicine, given to him formerly by a doctor, which was to be drunk mixed with human milk.

Vol 4 Page 59

. . . took down his trousers, lifted his penis, then ordered the woman to take it in her mouth, while he himself enjoyed the wine. "Suck this well for me" he said, "and I will give you an ornate gown to wear on festival day. "Certainly" answered the woman, "I wish to suck again and again . . . then took down his dress and trousers. The woman lay on the bed and Hsi-men took from the fold three bits of myrrh soaked in wine, which he had had from that time when he pleased himself with mistress Lin. He took down the woman's clothes and put some bits of myrrh on her breast, some on her stomach and some on her cunt. Then he set fire to all at once. He put his penis into her cunt, watching while the head was thrust in, and pushed himself fiercely. At last he took a mirror in order to see better and it was not a long time before the myrrh burned down near to the woman's skin, her eyebrows lifted, her teeth closed in greatest pain, at last in a trembling voice she said "Make an end, I am able to bear nothing more." . . . his penis was so long and so thick that it filled her cunt completely. Up and down they progressed, now the flower red like a parrot's tongue, now black like the wings of a bat It was pleasing and wonderful to see. He held her legs, their bodies pressed together, his penis went in deep to the very root The woman's eyes opened and the love juices flowed from her Hsi-men achieved the greatest desire and his semen flowed out like a river.

Vol 4 Page 82

Hsi-men Ch'ing visits Porphyry.

. . put it on his penis and tied the ends behind his body Then he drank the medicine mixed with wine. Porphyry stroked his penis and soon it arose proudly. The veins stood out and it seemed to be a liver purple He valued the silk ribbon much more than the clasp. Hsi-men Ch'ing lifted the woman above his knees and pushed his penis into her cunt. . . .

His penis was exceedingly hard He asked the woman to place her hands and legs in the position of a horse and he pushed himself into the flower from the rear. . . . He did this 150 times while he beat the woman's bottom with a loud noise. She, with her hands hanging down, played with the heart of the flower and called him endearing names unceasingly . . . Golden Dragon stretching its claws, and they urged themselves now this way, now that, one time going down from on high, another time making a short road. . . . As often as he drew out his penis, so often she restored it to the hilt herself and they did this 150 times

Vol 4 Page 83

. . Soon he drew it out entirely and he put a quanity of red powder on the end of his penis Then while he pushed himself again into her cunt, he tickled her so much that she was hardly able to endure it Lifting herself up she implored him to push deeper, but Hsi-men Ch'ing deliberately played at the vestibule, touching the heart of the flower softly for he did not wish to go deep Her love juices flowed like liquid from the ivy Under the light Hsi-men watched her white legs wrapped around both sides of his body. His own legs trembled as he saw her tremble Seeing this made him yet wilder.

112

Weary Hsi-men Ch'ing returns home from his visit to Porphyry. Not knowing of the monks warning that only one aphrodasical pill must be taken at a time, Golden Lotus gives three to Hsi-men Ch'ing and seals his doom.

She squeezed his penis, moved it up and down, and sucked it, but the head only drooped

Vol 4 Page 85

She put powder on top of his penis and inserted it into her cunt, the heart of the flower was penetrated without delay. . . . At first because of dryness it was difficult but soon the love juices flowing lubricated her cunt   . She twisted herself on the penis, which was all the way in her, only the two testicles remained outside   She pulled the penis with her hand, marvelling how good it looked   The juices flowed and in a short time consumed five napkins   Even then Hsi-men persevered, the head of his penis swelled and was hotter than glowing coal   It was so greatly constricted that he asked the Golden Lotus to remove the ribbon, but the penis remained rigid.   He asked her to suck it   She bent over and sucked the head with her red lips, moving it here and there   Suddenly white semen flowed, like quicksilver, which she took into her mouth but she was not able to drink it quickly enough   At first the semen was natural, but then blood flowed without stopping.

Vol 4 Page 92

The learned doctors theories, Hsi-men Ch'ings' penis remains rigid, attentions of his first wife, Moon Lady, bring no relief, but instead hasten his end.

Vol 4 Page 93

Hsi-men drank the medicine that was sent but his penis stood continuously as if made of iron. Through the night, the woman, not knowing how much harm it could do, got up on his body and played the game of the candle upside down

Vol 4 Page 145

In this excerpt we learn the names of instruments, though a much desired description of these instruments is lacking.   We are told that some marriage manuals contained two dozen pictures.

FELLATIO

The practice of applying the female mouth to the male organ has a place in the pattern of Chinese sex behavior as it does in the cultures of other peoples. Fellatio, however, was not meant to provide the male with full satisfaction, but merely to stimulate an erection and excite his desire as a prelude to normal intercourse.

It is interesting to note, as in this illustration, that the penis is never shown actually in the mouth of the female. The explanation of this peculiarity is that, by the accepted conventions of Chinese art, the female mouth should not be represented as large enough to hold the enlarged male organ.

This illustration, and the one following, are from a series of 36 painted on silk. To paint successfully on silk required a sure and skilled hand since there was no means of ready erasure. At times an outline was first sketched in pencil. The standing gentleman is a government official. His rank is indicated by the color of the stone in the center of his hat.

Size 8" x 9¼"

114

Many of the scenes illustrated in the Marriage Manuals are found in Ching Ping Mei, including the oft used ones of a servant physically assisting in the movements of the male participant.

Vol 4 Page 146

He arranged the warrior within the woman's cunt and progressing backwards and forwards furnished the greatest pleasure and gladness to both

Vol 4 Page 274

Ching-chi goes to Yen Kung monastery, becomes a priest and accepting homosexual attentions from the novice Chin Tsung-ming uses it as a weapon to ply the ancient art of blackmail.

Vol 4 Page 275

Ching-chi pressed his back against the belly of the monk, said nothing, and acted as though he were sleeping. The penis of the monk became rigid and rose like a spear. He placed spittle on it and rushed in. While Ching chi had been sporting among the beggars, two friends stretched his anus by evil use, so that the way was easy for the monk

RANDOM NOTES TO CHING PING MEI

During copulation there seemed to be no regard for the feelings of the female. Males appeared not disturbed by protestations and complaints of pain but proceed with their intentions. Hot wine was frequently drunk before the act.

Maid servants assisted in preliminary preparations of undressing and fixing the bed. Their presence and knowledge that the act of coition was taking place did not apparently disturb the romancers.

White skin was a desirable attribute in the female. Premarital relations practically in every incident preceded marriage. That a woman acquiesced before wedlock did not lesson her status in the man's estimation or act as a deterrent to marriage.

The silver clasp referred to was an instrument not unlike a safety pin which fastened at the root of the penis, restricted the flow of blood and unlimitedly retained erection. Finding the hard metal not too pleasant, Golden Lotus made a belt of soft cloth which in purpose accomplished the same function without annoyance to the female.

Rabelasian Humor

He is one of those men who can see a bee piddling forty miles away, but not an elephant outside their very own doors

If you want to see a slave you'd better piddle and look at your own image in the pool you make

Why must you use jasmine soap Is that why your face is cleaner than some people's bottoms?

Colorful Expressions

A tasty piece of lamb sometimes falls into a dog's mouth (A beautiful girl is sometimes married to a scrawny husband)

A beautiful horse is often ridden by some fool of a man (A pretty girl sleeping with a husband who is not fit to be seen)

He opens his eye, but not a word does he have to say for himself (a penis in erection)

RANDOM NOTES

FIVE ESSENTIAL QUALIFICATIONS OF A WIFE STEALER

He must be as handsome as P'an An

His member must be at least as large as a donkey's

He must be as rich as Teng T'ung

Reasonably young.

Plenty of time on his hands, and almost endless patience

KINDNESS

It would seem that in all the world there is not a single woman, no matter how intelligent she may be, who cannot be led astray by some trivial act of kindness. Nine women out of every ten are caught this way.

BEST AGE

The middle twenties is the age when a woman's beauty is at its loveliest and a man's vigour at its highest

The effete man was called a waxen spear-head, a dead turtle, an eel.

PROSTITUTION

There appeared to be no social stigma to prostitution. A prostitute was invited and visited in the home with wives whose husband showered attention on her

To visit a prostitute was socially accepted, but philandering with another man's wife would cause a family furor

Double Standard

After staying at a bawdy-house for several days teaching singing-girls the arts of love, and carousing in high spirits with some of his disreputable companions, Hsi-men Ch'ing returned home to celebrate his birthday When he learned that one of the servant boys had had an affair with Golden Lotus, his fifth wive, he flew into a towering rage, had the boy stripped and terribly beaten with a bamboo pole, and thrown out. He made his wife take off her clothes, kneel before him and he horse-whipped her.

Pessimistic Attitude to Marriage

Even the marriage most blessed by Fate seems full of evil.
Men in their folly crave for love, yet, when in calm collected-ness they study it, hateful it seems.

The gate of Love may be the gate of Life, but just as surely it is the gate of Death Time and time again our common sense reminds us of this fact, and yet our hearts still carry us away. So do men fall victims to the plague of love.

Those charming dainty maidens who serve our lusts so well, whose skill in self-adornment is so exquisite when once the veil is torn aside, what shall be find in them but falseness?

The silken hose, the tiny feet are like the pick and shovel that dig our graves Soft dalliance upon the pillow, the sport of love upon the bed, are but the forerunners of an eternity within the Fifth Abode of Hades, we shall be boiled in boiling oil.

Wife's comments to her inept husband

She snatched the poker from his hand and cried, "You don't know how to poke. Let me do it for you. I want it as hot as a bowl of fire."

Women Alike

As the proverb says, a young man is never faithful to one girl All the coins in the world are made with the same sort of hole I don't mean to boast, but my daughter is a good-looking girl Your own eyes, Sir, will tell you that much.

Maidenhead

Never laugh when you are swinging It makes the legs give way, and down you fall I remember when I was a girl Miss Chou while swinging was thrown off. She fell across the board and she broke her maiden head. Later, when she married, people said she was not a pure girl, and she was divorced.

AN EMPEROR'S DIVERTISSEMENT
(In author's collection)

Although the dividing line between fact and legend in such matters is difficult to determine, some of China's ancient emperors are reputed to have led sex lives as fabulous as they must have been demanding upon the imperial energies Sexual prowess was an admired characteristic of leadership Court custom prescribed that the emperor should spend two nights in every month with the empress and, in addition, give amorous attention at regular intervals to each of his concubines, who sometimes numbered—according to historical record—as many as three hundred To the non-understanding foreigner this illustration presents a rather humorous picture with its "Pillow of Flesh," but the Chinese saw in it the moral that the lot of an emperor's darling was not entirely a bed of roses For even if the emperor possessed the sexual stamina necessary to fulfill his amorous obligations, his many imperial concubines could hardly expect to receive all the attention they desired.

This brilliantly-colored painting on silk purports to show the Emperor Yeng of the Sui Dynasty, famed for his amorous proclivities, enjoying a visit to one of his concubines. As befits his imperial station, he remains fully garbed in majestic yellow robes and is being waited upon hand and foot Two concubines support him on either side, swaying him back and forth so that he need not exert himself. The amoret receiving his favor reclines on a couch, bracing herself against the soft body of one of the others and holding a tray with a cup of wine to offer to His Majesty

Chinese religion is more a liberal philosophy of life than the strict adherence to ritual performances, hence, at a funeral, priests of several beliefs may be present and officiate, thus a man may elect from different faiths that which, to his judgment was most acceptable

He may subscribe to the Taoists teaching that a woman during orgasm gives forth essence which the male absorbs during copulation This essence adds both to his strength and his years It causes gray hairs to turn black, new teeth to sprout on bare gums, and adds to the health of the child on those occasions when he ejaculates for purposes of procreation.

Ejaculation was to be avoided and the essence retained as much as possible except for fertilization By learning the correct technics of breathing he could restrain himself. Intercourse with as many women in one night as possible added to his strength, for woman was the source of energy The longer his penis remained in the vagina, the more essence he absorbed

In contrast to the philosophical concept of strength derived from intercourse is that of weakness The story, in which the Chinese must have taken much delight for it is oft repeated in various forms, of the gorgeous and desireable concubine who was given as a present to a despotic brigand general, who becomes so enamoured of her captivating charms that he gives to her increasingly of his attentions to the neglect of his military duties, and was thus easily vanquished

118

THE LADY OF THE MOON

The facing picture, and the six which immediately follow, are reproductions, in original size, of the illustrations for a Ming period novel **The Lady of the Moon.** They were engraved, circa 1610, by Huang I-chieh who may also have been the artist.

The authorship of the novel is not known, the only evidence available as to its origin is in the signature of the preface which is signed with a seal which means 'the immortal of the Square Pot.' This is a favorite symbol of the Taoists

Historical setting of the Novel

The action of the novel takes place during the latter years of the Ming dynasty when morals had declined to such a point that men were elevated to high office for their success in concocting aphrosdisiacs not, as in previous times, for their knowledge of the classics and for their scholarship During the reign of Chia Ching (1522-67) one T'ao Chung-wên was awarded the high rank of Secretary of the Board of Rites, Tutor to the Heir after he had ingratiated himself with the emperor by presenting him with his "Red Lead"

The example of the court was followed by painters and writers, erotic themes were freely treated in the art and literature of the time, and erotic novels and paintings came into vogue

Synopsis of the Story

The 'hero' of the story is Wu San-ssu, consort of Kao Taung of the T'ang dynasty, who usurped the throne and ruled for twenty years after her death Although he had a large harem, he was growing weary of his wives until he discovered among them a young girl whom he had not seen before Her charms soon captivated him completely Together they staged the 'forty-three forms' As they acted each 'form' one or the other gave it a name

Hearing of her exquisite beauty, the minister, Ti Jen-chieh, insisted upon seeing her She was reluctant, protesting that he was an upright man and that she was not a mortal but a spirit from the moon He persisted and was finally introduced to her As a result of their meeting the Moon Lady shortly afterwards ascended to another world taking with her the spiritual essence of Wu At a later time, visitors to the Chung Nan mountains reported seeing both of them as Taoists

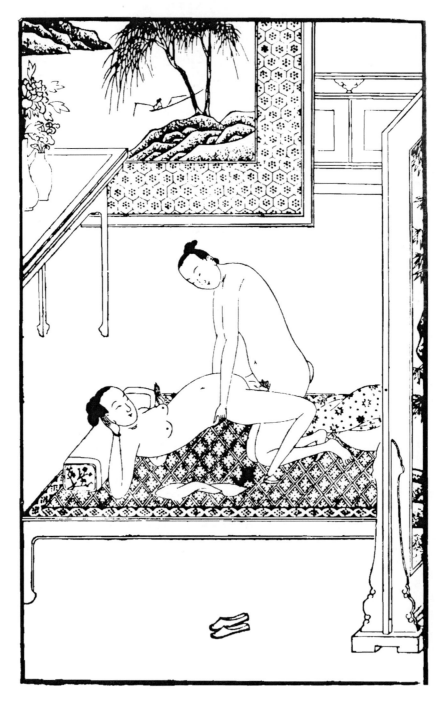

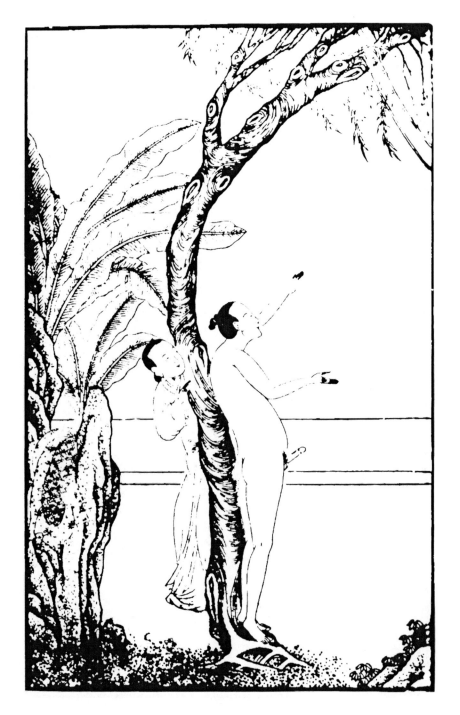

AMULETS

(Disks Surrounding Square Mirror)

Superstition, which finds a place in every ancient culture, has left behind its traces in many art forms, of which amulets are one. In China these were commonly fashioned of brass or bronze with a square hole in the center to permit them to be threaded on a string and worn about the person as a charm protecting the wearer against the evil influences of demons, against lightning, snake bites and other dangers, and bringing him instead good fortune, long life and numerous progeny. They were often inscribed with good wishes and presented to friends on birthdays, New Year's and other festive occasions.

There is a striking resemblance between amulets and coins. Some scholars maintain that coins derived from amulets, others that amulets derived from coins. Whichever may be the correct hypothesis, the existence of a close relationship is substantiated by the fact that amulets were sometimes used as money, while coins served as amulets.

The decorative motif was frequently of an erotic nature. The amulet shown here bears on one side the ideographs signifying Moon, Snow, Flower, Wind, and on the other four scenes of sexual intercourse. Moon, Snow, Flower and Wind represent the four seasons—autumn, winter, spring, summer—hence denoting the never-ending cycle of life and procreation. Even the round shape and square hole have a special connotation, for to the Chinese Heaven (round) was male, and Earth (square) was female. Their juxtaposition thus expresses the eternal union of the sexes, of **Yang** and **Yin.**

MIRROR BACK

Ming Period, 1369-1644

(Square Shaped Bronze Surrounded By Round Amulets)
2⅜ inches x 2⅜ inches

Since the art of glass-making was not indigenous, mirrors made of glass were not known in China before the arrival of the Dutch and Portuguese traders. Instead the Chinese used mirrors fashioned of cast bronze, the functional side being a smooth, polished surface while the back usually bore some kind of artistic decoration.

The square bronze piece in the center of the illustration is one of these ancient mirrors, showing the reverse side with its décor of four varied scenes of copulation. The design, though more elaborate, is similar to those of the surrounding amulets. In the middle of the mirror is a perforated knob through which a silken cord was passed to provide a means of holding it while in use.

Beside their normal function as an aid in dressing the hair, mirrors were commonly placed in the tombs of deceased persons as a protecting charm. The apex of the tomb was sealed with a brick set in mortar, and a mirror was fastened to the underside of the brick by means of an iron wire. Reflecting downward, the mirror was supposed to light the tomb and to dispel evil spirits and goblins, which would be frightened away by the sight of their own images.

Mirrors are still regarded as protective charms by the superstitious and are often hung in front of the bed curtains to ward off evil during the night.

BIBLIOGRAPHY

The Adventures of Hsi Men Ching, translated from the Chinese, illustrated in black and white New York Privately printed for the Library of Factious Lore 1927 Limited to 750 copies Translator's note signed Chu Tsui-Jen A condensation of The Golden Lotus Leaves much to be desired

Egerton, Clement (-) The Golden Lotus Published by Routledge & Kegan Paul Ltd, London 1939, and reprinted 1953 4 Vols A masterful translation done with skill and feeling Ching P'ing Mei at its best A five star reading must

Fornaro, Carlo (1871-) The Chinese Decameron N Y The Lotus Society 1929 Rendered into English by de Fornaro from the French of George Soulie De Morant Taken from 16th century novels.

Hackney, Louise W Guide-Posts of Chinese Painting Boston and New York 1929, pp 221. Sensitively written A charming storehouse of delightful information

Himes, Norman E Ph D Medical History of Contraception London 1936 pp 521

Hsu, Francis L K (-), Americans and Chinese Two ways of Life, New York 1953, pp, 457 Keen and refreshing observations

Latourette, Kenneth Scott (1884-) The Chinese, their History and Culture Third Edition Revised New York 1946, 847 pp Scholarly, worthy, reads easily

Lee, James Zee-Min (-) Chinese Potpourri, pp 329 Hongkong 1950 Contains much delightful information not found in other sources

Maspero, Henri (-) Le Taoisme pp 264 Civilisations Du Sud Paris 1950

Miall, Bernard, and Dr Franz Kuhn Chin P'ing Mei The adventurous History of Hsi Men and his six wives With an introduction by Arthur Waley New York 1947 pp 863 Translated from the Chinese into the German, and from the German into English Very good, has the Chinese flavor, but not complete

Needham, Joseph, F R S (1900-) Science and Civilisation in. China Vol 2 History of Scientific Thought Cambridge 1956, 697 pages Scholarly, thoroly annotated, intelligently liberal Excellent on Taoism

Smith, Arthur H, D D (-) Chinese Characteristics New York 1894, pp 342 After 22 years in China, the author, possibly a disappointed missionary, found everything to condemn and nothing to praise

Van Gulik, Robert Hans Erotic colored prints of the Ming period Published in Tokyo, 1951 An edition limited to 50 copies Original text all hand written and hand printed Exceptionally important For review see Asia Major New Series Vol 3, No 2, 1952.

CPSIA information can be obtained at www.ICGtesting.com
Printed in the USA
BVOW04s1452010315

389516BV00012B/167/P